The Boy Doctors Wrote Off

Doctors gave 4-year-old Ashley only months to live.

Andrew and Vivien Fowle's world collapsed when they were told their son Ashley had a large tumour on his spinal cord and brain stem. The doctors had tried everything, but nothing had stopped the tumour's spread.

Then, when she was at her lowest, Vivien read about a New York surgeon who operated on children like Ashley. Could an American doctor help when the NHS couldn't?

A transatlantic phone call to Dr Fred Epstein gave Andrew and Vivien hope, and within days they were raising the money for an amazing mission to save their son's life.

The Boy Doctors Wrote Off

Andrew & Vivien Fowle
Roger Day

A LION BOOK

Published by
Lion Publishing plc
Sandy Lane West, Oxford, England
ISBN 0 7459 3646 6
Albatross Books Pty Ltd
PO Box 320, Sutherland, NSW 2232, Australia
ISBN 0 7324 1493 8

First edition 1996
10 9 8 7 6 5 4 3 2 1 0

Printed and bound in Great Britain
by Cox & Wyman Ltd, Reading

Contents

Acknowledgements

We would like to acknowledge just a few of those who have been involved with us in helping to make this story possible, both in the UK and the US.

A big thank you to the thousands of people who gave sacrificially to the 'Ashley to America' appeal fund. Without their help this story would have been a very different one.

Thanks to Vivien's mother and father, Charlie and Ann, who were very supportive throughout the difficult times. Also thanks to Andrew's parents, Michael and Ann. Initially they were concerned at the speed of Fred Epstein's decision to operate in the US and questioned how he could decide when he hadn't even seen Ashley. After all, the British doctors at least knew him. Now Michael and Ann are so glad we went!

We are grateful to Jackie, Vivien's sister, for her support and her words of wisdom about Ashley that have helped us through difficult times. And how would we have managed without Angie, Andrew's sister? She showed such kindness and support as she looked after our other two children, Simon and Michelle, for two months while we were away.

We appreciate the way the Kent police have shown incredible support to us throughout the difficulties: Jan Berry, chair of Kent Police Federation and vice-chair of the Kent Police Benevolent Fund, who spearheaded and ran Ashley's appeal; Gill Clements of the Benevolent Fund, who launched Ashley's appeal fund and continues to administer it; Sue Roberton, the police welfare officer who travelled with us during our time in the US; Chief Superintendent Richard John Rixon, commanding officer at Maidstone Police Station where Andrew works, who was good enough to give him so much time off; and Peter Harman at Police Federation headquarters, the big, cuddly policeman who kept his eye on our other children while we were in the US.

Thanks are due to bank manager Bill Mennis, a great banking engineer if ever there was one. Rumour has it that he may even have bent and broken some rules in the interests of Ashley's appeal fund!

We are deeply grateful to Lee Rawlinson, our good friend and long-term babysitter.

A big thank you to Virgin boss Richard Branson and his staff at Virgin's head office. He gave us the tickets to fly to the US, then flew us back first class when he learned that Ashley was unable to sit for long periods. Thanks also to the flight crews both ways across the Atlantic.

Without hesitation on his part, Trevor Harrison of Stena Sealink rallied his company and raised a lot of money for Ashley's appeal fund. Thanks to Fred Stokes and all the crew on board Stena Challenger, who looked after us so well when we visited the ship as guests. Thanks to Stena Sealink for donating a day trip to France.

We appreciate BBC Radio Kent for its auction in aid of Ashley's appeal. Also thanks to West Ham United Football Club, and some of the other Premier League clubs, who donated signed shirts and footballs to the auction. Phil Collins helped drum up support by donating a set of signed drumsticks.

Dr Ian Millar, our family doctor, has been very understanding and helpful to us. So has Dr David Leung at the Livingstone Hospital in Dartford, who first suspected Ashley's condition and who instigated his initial referral to Guy's Hospital, London. We appreciate the help of the nursing staff and junior doctors at Guy's, who did a great job.

We are grateful to Paul Ki Ho Song, who approached us and asked to pray for Ashley, as he had been told there was something wrong with his head; Dave Webster, our pastor at Gravesend Christian Fellowship, who supported us and passed us on to a good church in New York; and Dave Walsh, who said he believed that Ashley's story would be a well documented and publicized one.

Thanks for the help and support of the Rainbow Trust, the charity for seriously ill or dying children, especially Tina Norris, the domiciliary care worker, who was a great friend in times of need.

We acknowledge the support of Raynehurst Infants School, where Ashley attends. Special thanks to the headteacher, Mrs Alison Whiting, and Ashley's teacher, Mrs Jane Bright, who had to endure the presence of the media in their school.

We are thrilled with all the help and support we've received from other families whose children have suffered tumours and cancer. It's impossible to mention them all, but the family we have come to know best are the Goulds, with whom we stayed in New York. Roger and Michelle and their daughter, Hollie, suffered just as much as brave young Jo Gould, with his highly malignant tumour, who kept his fighting spirit to the very end. Also thanks to Ray and Alison Barrett of the Alex Barrett Trust and to the memory of their son, Alex.

There are a number of people in the US we would like to thank. We are grateful to the folk at the New York Ronald McDonald House, who made us feel so much at home in the Big Apple. Thanks to Mike Turrigiano, pastor of the Manhattan/New York City Vineyard Church, his family and his church, who all welcomed us as their own.

We would like to thank several individuals in the US: Paul Strait, a good friend and rock in our time of need; Lauri Mah, who had so much faith and immediately saw hope for our Ashley; Nathan Bowie, who had a special bond with Ashley; Eric and Beth Kech, good friends who made great waffles; Rosanne Cicirello at the NatWest Bank US in New York, who was so understanding and for whom nothing seemed too much trouble; Christy Worsoe, physiotherapist at the New York University Medical Centre, for kick-starting Ashley after his operation and who gave him a lot of her spare time free of charge; and Lynn Odell, Press Officer at the Medical Centre, who coped marvellously, despite being inundated with calls from the Press about Ashley.

Thanks are due also to the Walt Disney World Company, especially Jayne Kear, and Tom and Debbie Marziale, who looked after us and treated us like royalty while we were in Florida.

Above all, we are indebted to Dr Fred Epstein of the New York University Medical Centre for his compassion, encouragement and unbelievably competent skills as a neurosurgeon. Without him there would be no story to tell.

Andrew and Vivien Fowle

In addition to many of the people already mentioned by Andrew and Vivien, I would like to thank my team of faithful readers, who made helpful comments at various stages in the writing of this book. My special thanks to Robin Gaulton, for willingly meeting such impossible deadlines, and to Tammy Wood, for her down-to-earth comments. I'm also grateful to my wife, Christine, my chief critic and greatest encourager.

Roger Day

Foreword

As someone with a sense of adventure I have faced death a number of times while crossing vast oceans or soaring to the dizzy heights in a flimsy hot-air balloon.

Like me, little Ashley Fowle is an adventurer. He has faced death many times in his young life, yet each time has soared above it. This book records the highs and lows of that battle for life. It's a story of tragedy and triumph. And, through it all, Ashley's sparkling sense of humour shines brightly.

When doctors told Ashley's parents he was going to die, they refused to give up. Against impossible odds, they heard about and contacted the only doctor in the world willing to help their son. Their determination to raise the needed money for a life-saving operation inspired a nation.

I feel privileged that we at Virgin have had a small but vital part in helping Ashley.

I recommend this book to all fellow-adventurers. Read it and discover hope even in the most difficult of situations.

Ashley's is an amazing story of courage that's an inspiration to us all.

Richard Branson
Chairman, Virgin Group

1 Tragedy Strikes Twice

The automatic sliding doors closed with a gentle swoosh and the three of them were inside.

The drab Victorian architecture of the main part of Guy's Hospital, London, contrasted with this modern extension next door to the hospital, known simply as The Tower. It was a familiar sight to the man and the woman. Ashley, the blond boy in the pushchair in front of them, had been in and out of hospital more times than they could remember in the three and a half years since he had been born.

This was just another of those appointments they had become so used to. Yet for some reason they couldn't really explain, Andrew and Vivien Fowle were dreading this appointment more than .any of the previous ones.

For one thing, Vivien disliked Professor James Richardson, the man they had come to see. Vivien, a mother of three with straight, blonde hair and glasses, hated the cold, clinical way in which he tended to talk about Ashley's medical condition.

For another thing, Professor Richardson was no ordinary doctor. He was a neurologist, specializing in problems associated with the brain and nervous system. That was enough to strike terror to the heart of any caring parent.

It was Tuesday, 29 March 1994 and Andrew and Vivien had come to find out the results of a biopsy of Ashley's brain stem—the tiny extension of the spinal cord that is the common pathway to all body functions, including blood pressure, heartbeat, movement and breathing. They also hoped to find out the results of a magnetic resonance imaging (MRI) scan that had been done on Ashley. The MRI scan shows the brain and spinal cord in 'slices'—magnetic pictures of different sections.

Doctors had done the scan and then decided to do a biopsy under general anaesthetic at the Maudsley Hospital, London, to find out why Ashley had always found walking such a task and was now experiencing difficulty moving his arms. He had developed an unexplained stiffness in his neck and, most worrying of all, the pupils of his eyes were sometimes different sizes.

The journey to the hospital had already been gruelling enough. The Fowle family lived in Northfleet, near Gravesend, Kent, and Andrew and Vivien had decided that travelling by train was the easiest way of getting into the heart of the capital.

With a 10 o'clock appointment they had to catch one of the many commuter trains that travel each day from Gravesend to London Bridge Railway Station. The actual journey time was only three-quarters of an hour but to them it seemed an eternity. They were crammed into the carriage like sardines, suffocating among the crowds of tired-looking business people, some still rubbing the sleep from their eyes. At least they were able to find some room in a no-smoking carriage so that the already stuffy air wasn't also thick with smoke.

At London Bridge they had been greeted by the hustle and bustle of London on a working weekday. Going through the abandoned ticket barrier was like negotiating whitewater rapids in a canoe in slow motion. Finally, they came out onto the streets of London and made their way through the noise and pollution to Guy's Hospital, which was conveniently only a couple of minutes' walk away.

Their appointment was in Ronnie MacKeith Ward, the venue for sick children and their parents on the tenth floor of The Tower. The elevator took them slowly past each floor, a computer voice announcing the wards and departments on that level.

'Ronnie MacKeith and Hector Cameron,' came the tinny voice as the elevator ground to a bumpy halt, and they emerged onto the tenth floor. Soon they were in the ward where the meeting would take place.

They reported to the ward nurses' station and then sat nearby, waiting to be seen, Ashley still in his pushchair. The nurses' station consisted of a desk, telephones and all the emergency bells from the ward. This was where any visitors reported. From it the nurses could see over the whole ward.

After a short wait they were approached by a slim, blonde-haired woman who introduced herself as Julie, the play specialist. She spoke with a broad Liverpudlian accent and had a bright, bubbly personality to go with it.

Julie looked at Ashley in his pushchair. 'Would you like to go into the toy room to play with some toys?' she asked him.

'Yes,' he said without a moment's hesitation.

Andrew and Vivien followed them in.

'What sort of things does Ashley like playing with?' Julie asked.

'He loves jigsaw puzzles,' said Vivien. 'In fact, he's almost addicted to them!'

'Good,' laughed Julie, 'because I've got lots of puzzles in my special cupboard.'

She pulled out a selection of puzzles and Ashley went straight for one of his favourites, a picture of Postman Pat, famous as the animated TV character.

A few minutes later Professor Richardson came into the room. With his bushy beard and above-average height he was the spitting image of Terry Waite (the former envoy of the Archbishop of Canterbury who had been held hostage for five years in Lebanon). After a brief chat, Professor Richardson suggested it would be best to leave Ashley in the playroom with Julie and go to a more private room where they wouldn't be disturbed.

They headed for the parents' rest room. This small room had been designed to give parents staying with their sick children on the ward a coffee break away from the tragedies they saw every day in the lives of little children, some of whom were dying of incurable diseases. It was a dark, depressing room, painted orange. Because it was in the centre of the building, there were no windows looking outside.

The room had a single coffee-table, a rack full of out-of-date magazines, an old TV set, a kettle and a few antiquated easy-chairs, relics of the 1960s. A plaque on the wall announced that the room had been furnished in memory of a child who had died of cancer.

Because of shortage of space on the ward, this room was often where the doctors broke bad news to parents. As a result it had come to be known as 'Death Row', and very few parents ever darkened its door voluntarily.

Andrew and Vivien followed Professor Richardson into Death Row. Behind them came several other people. There were three other doctors, Dr Elaine Hughes, Dr Joan Whitehead and a third doctor known simply as Dr Helen. At the back of the procession came Beth, popularly known as the tissue nurse. She solemnly bore a square box of paper handkerchiefs, much as a mediaeval priest would have borne the Bible behind the procession leading to an execution.

Vivien guessed straight away that there was something wrong. She felt as if she were going into the room for sentence to be passed on her. She was shaking like a leaf as if she had been freezing cold, even though the ward's central heating made it feel like a hothouse.

They sat in a circle. The tissues were put on the coffee table in the middle of the room, the box serving as a focal-point for Andrew and Vivien's attention.

Once everyone was comfortable Professor Richardson began. Andrew and Vivien sat glued to the spot in anticipation of what was about to be said.

'Those damned tissues,' thought Vivien. 'They can only mean one thing. Bad news.'

Professor Richardson held up Ashley's scans and explained what they had revealed. He pointed out a large tumour that extended from the brain stem at the base of his brain to the cervical spinal cord. This was confirmed by the results of the biopsy. Since birth Ashley had suffered from an unexplained build-up of fluid on his brain known as hydrocephalus.

'Looking at the scan when Ashley was eighteen months old, I'm pretty sure the original hydrocephalus was caused by the tumour blocking the flow of fluid,' said Professor Richardson. 'I think this tumour's been present since he was born.'

'How serious is it?' asked Andrew.

'It's not malignant like a cancer spreading through the body,' assured Professor Richardson. 'But if it goes on growing it could cause pressure on the sensitive structures of the brain. The fact that it's affecting his arms and legs is an indication of that.'

'What can be done to help him?'

'The tumour's growing only slowly, if at all. That leaves us with the question of whether we should do something about it now or watch him and repeat the scan in three months' time—or before, if there's a worry.

'There are three ways we can treat tumours: surgery, radiotherapy and chemotherapy. Chemotherapy involves injections and medication, something that kills the tumour cells.'

Professor Richardson explained that chemotherapy wasn't an option at the time because of where the tumour was situated. A new drug called Temozolamide was starting human trials the following month. If it got through the experimental stages, which would probably take four or five years, they would review Ashley's case to see if it could be used to treat him.

'Surgery isn't an option,' he continued gloomily. 'It's in the brain stem. We just can't do it.'

The third option was radiotherapy. Dr Joan Whitehead, the oncologist (cancer specialist), chipped in here. She explained what was involved in radiotherapy and about the many possible side effects. Radiotherapy would hopefully shrink the tumour into a dormant phase and preserve Ashley's quality of life.

They could start radiotherapy straight away or wait six months and do a fresh scan to see whether the tumour had changed. If there was any increase in the tumour's size, they would then have to start him on radiotherapy.

Assuming there was no change in six months they would wait another six months and do another scan. This would continue for as long as necessary.

If Ashley deteriorated in the next six months, Professor Richardson said he couldn't guarantee that radiotherapy would reverse any new symptoms he developed meanwhile.

'Do you believe the tumour will eventually cause Ashley's death?' asked Andrew hesitantly.

'I believe so, eventually. Yes.'

It was difficult for either Andrew or Vivien to believe what they had just heard. People don't go around telling parents their child is going to die. The neurologist couldn't be talking about their son.

Andrew felt like a zombie. What could he do? There was his little son back in the playroom contentedly doing jigsaw puzzles and they as parents had to go out and face him as if everything was still the same.

For Vivien, the reply cut deep inside. She felt as if someone had come up and smashed her in the face. The rest of the discussion was just a blur to her. She was going to lose her precious little son. She kept picturing his happy face, and the more she pictured him the more she wept. *'How am I going to look at Ashley now?'* she thought.

'You've put me on Death Row,' Vivien said bitterly. If Ashley was going to die, she would die, too.

With that, she could contain herself no longer. The tears streamed from her as she cried uncontrollably. It was the sign for the tissue nurse to come into action.

'How long has he got to live?' Andrew asked above his wife's crying.

'We're probably talking in terms of years rather than months. As a ball park figure I'd say he has five years.'

Five years! That meant Ashley was unlikely to see even his ninth birthday.

Professor Richardson had seemed so cold and apparently indifferent in passing sentence on Ashley. As a policeman Andrew understood how important it was for a person to become detached from his or her emotions in order to get on with the job in hand. He had been on the scene of fatal road accidents, suicides and other sudden deaths. He had learned to switch off his emotions in those situations. Similarly, he concluded, Professor Richardson had detached himself from the emotion of the moment in order to get on with the job in hand.

'We need to give Ashley the best quality of life for as long as we can,' the doctor continued.

'From what I hear, you'd prefer to start radiotherapy as soon as possible?'

'Yes. Our best chance of keeping him as good as we can for as long as we can probably comes from giving him radiotherapy now. If we wait until he's older and he gets weaker, we may not be able to reverse that with radiotherapy.'

Professor Richardson then got up and left them in the room to decide which way they wanted to go. But what was there to think about? Andrew and Vivien could only be guided by Professor Richardson's recommendations. Who were they to turn round and say: 'Don't do it'?

Andrew and Vivien sat for ten minutes or so in the room, with Nurse Beth and Dr Elaine Hughes trying to comfort them. Andrew had his arm around his wife in stunned silence. What were they going to do? How were they going to walk out of that room and face their little boy?

Eventually they got up and began what they later described as the hardest thing they had ever done—walk out of the room along the corridor, past all the other parents, nurses and children, towards their little son in the playroom. Professor Richardson and Dr Joan Whitehead were standing next to the nurses' station talking to each other as if everything was just fine. Andrew and Vivien passed them in silence and walked towards the playroom, directly opposite.

As they approached the room their hearts sank further and further. Vivien turned away at the last moment and stayed just outside, staring through a window overlooking London. Andrew went into the playroom.

Ashley was happily doing a puzzle with Julie. He glanced up and said: 'Look, Dad. Come here and see this puzzle.'

It was all just too much for Andrew. Tears welled up in his eyes and he could hardly contain himself. He bent his tall, lean frame, eyes filling with tears, and buried his face into little Ashley's back. He wept, trying hard not to let anyone see or hear, least of all his dying son.

Taking a deep breath Andrew regained control, at least temporarily. 'Come on, Ashley,' he said. 'Let's get your coat on and go home.'

Andrew struggled to put Ashley's coat on him but he could hardly see through his tears. It was an easy job he did almost every day, yet he was finding it impossible now. The minutes passed and still Andrew struggled to get the coat on his son. He felt totally alone, as if the bottom had dropped out of his world.

'Come on, Daddy. Hurry up,' Ashley said cheerfully.

That made things even worse.

Professor Richardson had obviously seen what was happening and had silently walked round behind Andrew to give him a reassuring pat on the shoulder. It was his way of trying to comfort Ashley's dad.

With Ashley's coat finally zipped up, Andrew regained his composure, picked up his son and put him in the pushchair. At the nurses' station he said to Professor Richardson: 'We'll go home, have a think about things and come back to you with our decision in the next week.'

'OK, goodbye.'

They had already made up their minds to go ahead with the radiotherapy treatment. Even though it sounded so drastic, it was their only hope.

They left the hospital, Ashley in his pushchair and his parents walking along behind. Out on the street heading for London Bridge station they passed crowds of people milling about in the early spring sunshine. Yet they felt totally alone.

The train ride home was one of the worst journeys they had ever made. Andrew and Vivien sat deep in their own individual thoughts. Ashley was on Andrew's lap, happily chattering away, oblivious to the devastating news his parents had just heard about him. It made the tragic news even more difficult to grasp.

They sat in silence, not knowing what to say to each other. Although the train was crowded, they each felt like the loneliest person on earth. There was no one to turn to and no one else knew what they were going through.

Most parents never face the tragic death of their child. Yet for Andrew and Vivien this was the second time tragedy had struck. Ten years previously they had been faced with another tragedy involving their firstborn child, Elizabeth.

2 Sudden Shock

When Elizabeth Anne Louise was born to Andrew and Vivien on 1 February 1984 she was the pride of both her parents. For Andrew she was at last a stabilizing influence in his storm-tossed life.

The oldest child of loving parents, Andrew's claim to fame was that he had won £28,000 on the soccer pools when he was only three years old. He had chosen the winning numbers and there was a family picture of him holding the winning coupon, his proud parents on either side of him. As a result of the win, the family moved upmarket to Carshalton, Surrey. Andrew had a younger brother, Duncan, and a sister, Angie.

Andrew had loved the sea from when he was very young. The Fowles had an old lifeboat and Andrew used to go sea-fishing in it. His father had been in the Royal Navy and had then worked in the pilotage service. So, at the age of twelve, Andrew followed in the family tradition and joined the Sea Cadets. He went in for sailing competitions and became coxswain of the Sea Cadet rowing team. He also joined the unit's band, playing side drum.

June 1976 was one of the hottest months on record. On one of the hottest days that month Andrew's band happened to be in a competition at RAF Henlow, Bedfordshire. They were dressed in full Royal Navy Number One uniforms, which were incredibly hot. They had to stand to attention for what seemed like hours, their instruments on the ground.

Suddenly, Andrew fainted, falling over and hitting his head on the brass tuning knobs of his side drum. He woke up in the medical room, having had five stitches put in his jaw. The scar remains to this day.

It was the start of a whole series of accidents over the next few years. Two weeks after fainting he was knocked off his bike and broke his ankle. He spent the entire school summer holiday, with his leg in plaster.

He and another Sea Cadet, David Shepherd, went to Walton on the Naze in Essex to try out a brand new Express sailing dinghy. The sea was rough at first but seemed to calm down when the tide turned. They launched the dinghy and were about 150 metres from shore when it capsized. That was no problem; they had mastered capsize drill so well that they could right a dinghy and somehow remain dry. This time, though, the mast had caught on the sand of the sea bed and they were being swept out to sea. Within minutes they were a mile and a half from shore.

Eventually a fishing boat came across them. The fifteen-minute trip to the coastguard station in biting cold winds left Andrew and his friend suffering from hypothermia. At the hospital, a doctor said that if they had been in the water for a couple more minutes they would almost certainly have died.

The dinghy was recovered, but the mast had pierced the hull. It was damaged beyond repair, but at least the two boys survived.

Another accident nearly stopped Andrew from becoming a sailor. Just before he started sea school at sixteen he rode up the kerb on his bike and the front wheel suddenly came off. He fell on his arm and ended up with a hairline crack up the entire length of the humerus bone in his upper arm.

After fourteen weeks at sea school in Gravesend, he got a job with the Merchant Navy, working for a company called Everards. He started as a deck boy and was soon promoted to able seaman. Quickly he was thrust into the tough adult world of wine, women and song. He had more money than he'd ever had before, and he soon learned how to enjoy himself to the full.

Drink, then more drink, quickly became the pattern. He lost count of the times he was carried back to the ship in a state of drunken unconsciousness, only to wake up the next day with a massive hangover and feeling sick. 'Never again,' he would say. But the next night he would be back drinking, then regretting it the following morning.

One time, his ship was in the port of Archangel, in the White Sea north of Russia, to pick up a load of timber. The sailors were escorted everywhere by Red Army conscripts, who also guarded the ship to prevent defectors. Apart from an Intourist guided visit to the town's Eternal Flame, the only place they were allowed to go to was the Seamen's Mission.

At the Mission, Andrew and his Scottish friend, Jimmy, had too many vodkas. They crept aboard another ship and drank themselves to sleep. At five o'clock the next morning, an armed guard frogmarched them back to their own ship. They sang rude songs about Russia on the way, thinking the guards couldn't understand.

On Monday morning they were visited by two KGB officers, taken to the rundown police station and interrogated.

'What happened on Friday night?' the commandant asked. 'I want you to write it down.'

'I don't know,' said Andrew. 'I had too many Russian vodkas.'

'This is bad. If you don't tell us we'll have to shoot you.'

'But I was drunk.'

'If you still can't remember, we'll put you in prison for ten years.'

In the end Andrew got some details from Jimmy and wrote it down. They were fined the equivalent of £37 and banned from visiting Russia.

After discharging the timber cargo in Holland, the ship returned to Archangel. Andrew and Jimmy got drunk on board ship and again made fun of Russia in front of the guards.

They were hauled in front of another commandant, who banned them from Russia for life. 'If you ever return you will be imprisoned for ten years,' he said. 'And I hope England doesn't win the World Cup.'

Later, on board ship, they watched on Soviet TV as Russia won the 1982 soccer World Cup. When they got back to the West, they were amazed to find that Russia hadn't even figured in the finals. Italy had scored 3:1 against West Germany. Soviet TV had distorted the event.

More than once, drink nearly cost Andrew his life. One time he was drinking lager in a seamen's bar in Europort, Rotterdam, talking with a pleasant Dutch couple.

'Have you ever tried geneva gin?' the man asked.

'No.'

'Right, I'll introduce you.'

The man produced a couple of tiny glasses and filled them with geneva gin. The idea was to drink the whole lot down in one gulp, then have a beer chaser to take away the revolting taste.

Andrew drank the gin, gasped for breath as the fire hit his throat, then gulped down some lager. He did this several times. After four or five geneva gins followed by beer chasers he couldn't remember much. He vaguely recalled going to a disco and then catching a taxi back to the ship at about two in the morning.

He was woken by the first mate at ten o'clock the next morning. He was fully clothed in cowboy boots, jeans and teeshirt. But he was dripping wet and the bedclothes were completely soaked.

'What's all this?' he asked, looking at his clothes and shivering.

The first mate explained that Andrew had got out of the taxi and staggered towards the ship. Somehow in his drunken state he had tripped over the small protective fence at the edge of the dock, rolled down the slope and straight into the deep water.

Andrew's drinking friend from the ship, who was also drunk, had gone to the ship and woken the steward. The steward had leapt into the water, dragged Andrew out, carried him on his shoulder like a sack of potatoes and plonked him down on his bed.

Another time Andrew's ship docked at Greenhithe, on the Thames just below London. A friend of Andrew's had glandular fever and a group from the ship went to visit him in hospital. While they were there they were invited into the staff bar. The seamen got into a drinking competition with the doctors. They lined up Bacardis on the counter and had a competition to see who could drink them the fastest.

After closing time, Andrew decided to walk back to the ship to sober himself up. By the time he got to the quay it was two o'clock in the morning. The last boat out to where the ship was moored had gone at 11.30. He decided to walk around the dock until the first boat went in the morning.

After a while, he stopped at the dock gate and spoke to a security guard.

'I know where you can sleep for the night,' the guard said. 'The dockers' canteen is near here. You're not supposed to go in there, but I can open it up and you can sleep on the sofa.'

'OK.' Andrew was grateful that he would be able to get his head down for a few hours while he waited.

'I'll wake you at six in the morning in time to catch the first boat.'

'Thanks.'

Andrew went into the canteen, a prefabricated building, and the security guard locked the door behind him.

Andrew lay back to wait for early morning, lighting a cigarette to help him relax. He must have dropped off to sleep because the next thing he knew was waking up to a sudden booming sound as the sofa burst into flames. He leapt up and tried to put out the fire by smothering it with cushions. That made matters worse. The fire had taken hold and already the room was full of thick, black smoke.

He tried the door but it had been locked from the outside. In panic he searched for a way of escape. At last he found it. He climbed up onto the sink and squeezed through a fanlight window. He was so shaken up by what had happened that he just ran and ran. Then, a few minutes later, he heard the fire engine arriving.

After he had walked around for a while to clear his head he went back to the dock gate. The security guard thought Andrew was a ghost! He had seen the flames and had gone into the canteen to search for Andrew. By then the sofa was engulfed in flames and he had thought Andrew was dead.

Another time Andrew was on a ship travelling from Rotterdam to the Thames with a cargo of soya beans. They were coming out of Rotterdam into a violent north-easterly storm. Winds from that direction come down the North Sea along the Norwegian coast and are funnelled into the English Channel. It is extremely cold and a very frightening experience even for seasoned sailors.

When they faced a storm at sea the sailors would wrap rags around the anchor chain and put a cement block over the chain locker entrance. This would usually keep out the sea water. Unfortunately, the ship had recently been in dry dock and one of the bolts holding the plate covering the entrance to the chain locker had been left off. The chain locker filled with water. This locker led into the fo'c'sle, where the paint, wire and ropes were stored.

There was a hatch leading from the fo'c'sle down into another storeroom. They forgot to shut this hatch and by the time they reached the Thames the whole front of the ship was down in the water. The fo'c'sle and storeroom had filled up. If the door into the main hold had been left open, water would have gone into the beans, which would have swollen and the ship would have sunk like a stone.

In all four of these situations Andrew knew he should have been dead. For some reason he had been spared. Somebody, somewhere, he felt, must have wanted him alive.

During this time he had no real friends, only 'Board of Trade mates'—friends on board ship who, when they returned to port, would never see each other again. In reality Andrew was lonely, and alcohol was his way of escape.

Things began to change after he got to know Vivien. They had first met while he was at sea school, and they had started going out with each other then. When he was at sea he would often be away four or five months at a time, so it was difficult to keep a relationship going.

He felt it was unfair to Vivien being away so long. One day he rang her up and said simply: 'I think it's time we stopped seeing each other.'

Despite that, she continued writing to him regularly. There was always a spark of love, and the letters tended to fan it into flames.

It was around this time that Andrew realized what a mess he had made of things. Vivien was a good sort who went to a church in Gravesend and she started to put him back on the straight and narrow. As a child he had been sent to Sunday school, mainly so his parents could have some peace and quiet on Sunday afternoons in front of the TV without the children bothering them. For Andrew, Sunday school had been a total bore, but it must have had some long-term effect. Now, although he didn't stop drinking, he certainly cut down enormously.

With love blossoming between them, life had a new meaning for Andrew. He had something to look forward to when he went on home leave. Eventually, on 11 December 1982, Andrew and Vivien got married at St Mary Magdalene Church in Frinton-on-Sea, Essex.

Marriage for Vivien was a chance to settle down after a fairly traumatic upbringing. For much of Vivien's childhood, her mother had suffered ill health. She had had a brain haemorrhage and then became a long-term user of antidepressants. This meant she had a Jekyll-and-Hyde personality. One day she could be very loving and seemed to be the best mother in the world. The next day she would be the total opposite.

Each day the three sisters—Fiona, Vivien and Jackie—would wonder which side of their mother they would see when they got home from school. Their mother was extremely house-proud and the girls had to learn to keep things immaculately tidy.

When Vivien was five the family went on holiday to Spain. Her mother told her over and over again: 'You mustn't eat Spanish ice-cream because you can get very sick from it.'

They were walking as a family through a Spanish market. Suddenly, little Vivien turned round and her parents weren't there. She started looking and crying and still no parents. 'I'm going to be lost here for ever,' she sobbed miserably.

Then a woman took her by the hand and led her to a policemen who in turn took her to the police station. One of the first things he said was: 'Do you want an ice-cream?'

'Yeah!' she said excitedly.

She sat on some steps eating her ice-cream. She decided to spin things out so that when her sisters showed up they would see her eating the ice-cream and be jealous. It seemed like hours, but she still had her ice-cream when they arrived—and despite her mother's warnings she never got sick!

Another time, Vivien's next-door neighbours were going on holiday and told her parents they had stacked up some hay in their garden and didn't want it touched. One day Vivien and her younger sister, Jackie, felt really mischievous. They decided to sneak next door and throw the whole lot all over the garden.

On the night when the neighbours were due to come back, Vivien and Jackie couldn't sleep with worry. At about midnight the neighbour banged on the door.

'Have you seen the state of my garden?' he shouted.

'No!' said Vivien's mother defensively.

'Well, come and look at it—now!'

'It's a bit dark. Can't we leave it until the morning?'

'I want you to see it *now!*'

Their mother went next door but Vivien and Jackie never heard any more about the incident. Incredibly, they didn't even get a telling off.

When Vivien was thirteen they went on a family holiday to Scotland, staying in a mobile home on a camping site. The three girls used to love to buy ice-creams and sweets from the all-night shop late at night. They would wait until the shopkeeper was in bed, then knock on the door. He would have to get out of bed to serve them and they would have great fun chanting the ritual as he served them yet another ice-cream: *'On goes the light. Up goes the lid. In goes the hand.'*

Vivien's first job was as a window dresser in a clothing store. She then became a shoe sales assistant. Things were unsettling at home and at the age of eighteen Vivien managed to escape the tension by getting a job as a live-in nanny to two little Asian children.

A while after Andrew and Vivien were married, Vivien started going along regularly to Frinton Free Church. She had always believed in God. As children, Vivien and her sisters—like Andrew—had been sent to Sunday school each week. Vivien felt it was her parents' way of getting rid of them for a while. As a fifteen-year-old she had started attending the local Mormon church. This was because, at the time, she was a devoted fan of the Osmonds, who were themselves Mormons. Now, though, she began to enjoy the services at the Free Church.

Andrew didn't share Vivien's enthusiasm for church. In July 1983, Andrew was packing his suitcase to go to sea yet again. Vivien was a couple of months pregnant at the time. Andrew came across a Bible that had been given to him at Sunday school. As he thumbed through its pages, the few happy memories of Sunday school came flooding back to him, so he threw it into his suitcase.

Once on board ship he began to read two or three chapters a day just before he went to sleep. It wasn't long before he had read the whole of the New Testament. He was struck by the fact that, although it had been written nearly two thousand years ago, it seemed so relevant to his life.

One night alone in his cabin Andrew did something he hadn't done since school assembly. He prayed. He simply asked Jesus Christ to come into his life. He asked God's forgiveness for his wrongdoing, even the things he couldn't remember doing when he was so drunk. As he lay on his bed he had a tingling sensation, starting in his feet and continuing up to the top of his head. It felt as if he were being dipped feet first into refreshing, warm water. His old selfish life had gone; he had been reborn into God's family.

After that, he began to pray every day about his home and his job. As he prayed he realized he wanted a job closer to home so he didn't have to be away from his wife and soon-to-be-born child. About a week before leaving the ship, he phoned Vivien and heard there was a job vacancy as a kitchen porter at a nearby Essex Voluntary Association for the Blind residential home.

He contacted the housekeeper, Mrs Turner, and explained his situation. To his surprise Mrs Turner kept the vacancy open until his ship came into port. He went for the interview and got the job. Although the money was a pittance compared with what he had been earning, life was much happier. He and Vivien were over the moon.

From then on both Andrew and Vivien went regularly to the Free Church, where they began to make friends.

Towards the end of her pregnancy Vivien developed *toxic pre-eclampsia*, a condition that affects one in twenty women, especially with first-time pregnancies. Although no one knows what causes this problem, doctors think it's related to decreased flow of blood in the placenta. Vivien's hands and face began to swell up, she put on weight rapidly and her blood pressure started to rise. A routine test also showed the presence of an abnormally high amount of protein in her urine.

She was rushed into Colchester Maternity Hospital and, after an emergency Caesarean, Elizabeth was born. Their lovely new baby weighed in at 7lb 5^1/$_2$oz (3.32kg). Apart from an extra finger on one hand, she was perfect. Andrew, unfortunately, wasn't able to be there at the birth.

Although they were both delighted with their new little daughter, Vivien suffered badly with post-natal depression. In addition, they had problems feeding Elizabeth. She was always bringing up her milk. As a result she tended to be on the small side and didn't put on much weight. Vivien had started off breastfeeding Elizabeth but was never sure how much she was getting. Even with a bottle, it took about an hour to feed her and then she would bring it all up again. There hardly seemed to be any time between feeds.

The hospital did a couple of investigations but could find nothing wrong with her. She was quite floppy and when Andrew and Vivien laid her down to sleep, she would often just lie there motionless.

They moved into a larger rented apartment and, once it had been decorated, they were able to relax as a family. Life wasn't without its problems, though, mainly through lack of money.

Once, they received a winter quarterly electricity bill for £100 when they didn't have the money to pay it. They prayed, asking God for guidance and a solution to their problem. A few days later Andrew had a phone call from Vivien while he was at work. A letter had arrived that morning with a cheque enclosed for £100. They had won the premium bonds.

Andrew had had those bonds since he was three years old and had never won a penny. Then, when he and Vivien were in trouble financially, they had won exactly what they needed, not a penny more or a penny less.

One night in June 1984 Andrew came in late and, as usual, bottle-fed Elizabeth. After feeding and changing her, he carefully laid the baby in her cot. She was instantly sick, soaking her clothes and bedding. Patiently, Andrew changed everything, put her to bed—and she did the same thing again. By now it was one o'clock in the morning and, after changing the bedding for the third time, he collapsed into bed, exhausted.

The next morning he was up late. He rushed into

the bathroom, had a quick wash and then raced out of the door. It was a thirty-minute walk to work and he half-walked and half-ran that morning so he wouldn't be too late.

Almost as soon as he got through the door of the residential home there was a phone call for him with Vivien at the other end of the line.

'The baby's dead! The baby's dead!' screamed Vivien hysterically.

Andrew was stunned into silence. He put the phone down.

'My baby's just died,' he told his shocked work colleagues.

They insisted on giving him a ride straight home. Andrew's dad was already there. So was Vivien's sister, Jackie, who had been staying with them for a few days.

Andrew's little daughter Elizabeth was lying on the bedroom floor, Andrew's dad trying desperately to resuscitate her. As soon as he saw her Andrew knew his baby was dead. So too had Vivien when she had walked into the little girl's bedroom. She had picked up little Elizabeth, who was totally limp. Vivien had gone screaming to her sister.

The ambulance arrived and, after a brief examination of Elizabeth's body, the ambulance crew left empty-handed. Then the police detectives arrived and sealed off the room. Although it was obviously a cot death, there was still the need for a thorough investigation. Eventually, when the police had finished their gruesome task, the undertakers arrived to take away little Elizabeth's body.

Sudden Infant Death Syndrome is the term they used to describe her death. Andrew and Vivien were absolutely devastated. Because there were no suspicious circumstances, there was no need for an inquest. Instead, an inquiry was held, the conclusion of which was that little Elizabeth had died of natural causes. Someone described it to them as a bit like the electrical supply being cut off by someone pulling out the plug.

For a long time Andrew blamed himself for Elizabeth's death. If only he had checked her in the night, he thought, she might not have died. Had she rolled over and choked on her own vomit after he had put her to bed for the third time?

Elizabeth was just four and a half months old when she died on 13 June 1984. That same evening Vivien was admitted to hospital in a state of total shock. After a series of tests, they told her that she was pregnant again.

While most parents would have expressed some feeling about such news, Vivien had run out of feelings. The fact that her precious baby had just died overwhelmed her. Instead of rejoicing at the news of her pregnancy, she broke down and wept.

3 Miracle Baby

Andrew and Vivien's dearly loved baby Elizabeth was buried in Kirby Cross, near Frinton-on-Sea, Essex.

Life had to go on, and they needed to start thinking about the new baby coming along. Yet, over and over, they kept asking the same question: 'Why, God, did you give us a precious child, then let her die four and a half months later?'

They continued to attend church regularly, but in the end they felt they were being hypocritical. There they were in church, singing praises to the King of kings, when inside they were hurting, angry and blaming God for taking their little girl from them.

'What loving father would give something as precious as a baby and then take her away again?' they asked bitterly. It was like buying your children their favourite sweets, then eating those sweets yourself in front of them.

'If you're going to be like that to me, I don't want to know you,' Andrew prayed through gritted teeth one day. With anger reaching bursting point within him, he bellowed out: 'Up yours, God.'

After that, Andrew and Vivien stopped going to Frinton Free Church. The church people tried to get alongside them, but with little success. Their good friends Pat and Sandy Burnett were a help during this difficult time. Pat had been Andrew's woodwork teacher at school and had seen him grow up and then commit his life to God. Now everything seemed in ruins.

Meanwhile, Simon Robert Andrew was born on 23 January 1985. He was much bigger than Elizabeth, weighing 8lb 9oz (3.88kg). At first, Vivien found it hard to bond with Simon because she was still mourning the loss of Elizabeth. She also put on a lot of weight, going up to 15st (186kg) in weight. There was one consolation. Unlike when she had

Elizabeth, she didn't suffer post-natal depression after Simon's birth.

Andrew and Vivien were involved at the time with the Sudden Infant Death Syndrome campaign and were given the option of being loaned a set of weighing scales or an *apnoea* alarm to check on Simon's breathing. One of the worst decisions of their lives was choosing the scales. They had to check and record Simon's weight every day. With the problems they had experienced in feeding Elizabeth they soon became paranoid about the normal loss of a few grammes in body weight soon after birth.

'He's going to die,' Vivien would say. She would sit up for an hour and a half at night making sure he finished every single drop of milk in his bottle. 'I don't want him to die on me,' she would say to Andrew.

At times Andrew and Vivien's relationship became very up and down because of the difficulties they had to face in coping with both a cot death and a second baby. They would argue over the least thing. Once Vivien took Simon in the carrycot and fled to her parents' house. Eventually, she returned and they made up. But the storm was always brewing just beneath the surface.

Over the months and years that followed, Vivien sought to make up to Simon for the difficulty she had in bonding with him during those difficult early months. Simon has always struggled with his school work. But he has made up for this in his enthusiasm for sport and his remarkable ability to remember things.

One night when he was only eighteen months old Simon barged into his parents' bedroom during one of their most intimate times. They shooed him out, vowing never again to let themselves be caught out by the children. Years later the Fowle children were staying with their grandparents.

At the end of the weekend Grandma said to Andrew and Vivian: 'What *are* you letting your children see?'

'What do you mean?'

'You know—sex and all that.'

'Don't be silly, Mum. We'd never...'

Grandma then recounted what she had heard. 'And to think that came from a seven-year-old!'

'But, Mum, he was only eighteen months when he saw that!'

Simon has always loved the beach and is familiar with many seaside areas within easy reach of their home. One time when he was nine, Simon and his family were playing with a ball by a tidal stretch of the River Thames at Gravesend. The wind caught the ball and it landed near the water's edge. Thinking it was on wet sand Simon raced towards the ball.

Suddenly he found himself sinking into black, muddy silt. By the time he was pulled out he was covered from head to foot in mud, looking like a creature from the black lagoon. Only a tuft of blond hair on top of his head was clean. He was crying, but Vivien was in tears of helpless laughter at the sight.

The mud stuck to him like glue. Vivien tried to catch the bus home but the bus driver took one look at Simon and drove off without them. Simon squelched the two miles home, leaving a trail of mud behind him. People were staring in utter amazement.

As Simon grew older he had a habit of losing some of his clothes on the beach. Once he came home on the bus from a day trip to Sheerness insisting on wearing one shoe, leaving the other lost in the sand for some beachcomber to find. Another time in Margate he lost his trousers. There was nowhere open to buy another pair so Simon travelled home in his underpants, constantly pulling his teeshirt down to avoid embarrassment.

Meanwhile, Andrew's job as a kitchen porter was becoming too much. It was a lot of hard work for very little money. He began to explore other avenues. He loved cooking and began to dream of the day when he could rise through the ranks of the kitchen hierarchy by becoming a chef. He was about to start an apprentice chef's course when his dad approached him.

'Look, there's a job going at Trinity House where I work. How do you fancy it?'

The result was that Andrew went back to sea, working with Trinity House Pilotage Service. It was much better money than he earned as a kitchen porter and, unlike the Merchant Navy, there wasn't the problem of being away from home for weeks or even months at a time.

When any ship comes into or out of port it needs an experienced local pilot to steer it through the narrow channels. Pilots know the sandbanks and currents very well. Andrew's job was to work on boats that took the pilots out to ships, then to bring them back again after they had finished their work. He worked out of Harwich, around the area of the Sunk Lightship.

Michelle Anna Claire came along on 29 January 1988. She was born by Caesarean section, weighed 7lb $7^1/_2$oz (3.39kg) and was uncannily similar in appearance to Elizabeth. Appearance wasn't the only similarity. One time when Michelle was just five months old, she started making strange grunting noises while she was in her baby buggy. Andrew and Vivien thought she was going to die. Terrified, they took her to hospital immediately.

'Things don't look good, I'm afraid,' one doctor told them gloomily.

The doctors put her on an antibiotic drip and kept her in hospital. Andrew and Vivien lived in fear that another daughter would go the same way as Elizabeth. But after a week she pulled through, none the worse for her ordeal. Whatever her illness, it never recurred. In fact, since then she has had hardly a day's illness.

Another scare happened when Michelle was eighteen months old. One day Vivien opened a bottle of baby food and was shocked to find broken glass in it. It was a time when extremist pressure groups were spiking baby foods with broken glass. The newspapers got hold of the story and soon there were photographs and headline stories of what might have happened.

Michelle was quite a character. Once she took her plate of food and put it upside down on top of her head, then laughed like a drain. She was the kind of child who could cope with the most difficult of circumstances. As a two-year-old she was walking through a supermarket one day when suddenly her panties fell down. Typically, she carried on walking as if nothing had happened, her panties draped unceremoniously around her ankles.

She also had a healthy appetite. A year or two after the supermarket incident her mother cooked a plateful of tiny sausages ready for a birthday party and left them on the kitchen table to cool. When she came back to the kitchen a while later there were only three left. For some reason little Michelle wasn't very hungry when it was time for the party food!

One year Simon and Michelle went with their grandparents to Grand Canaria in the Canary Islands. They had a wonderful time and the holiday gave their parents a welcome break. Simon won an art competition and Michelle got a certificate for her singing ability.

Michelle has always loved dolls and has managed to accumulate dozens over the years. She's also been good at pulling their heads off! She shares with her mother a secret passion for drawing chalks, that old favourite of pregnant mothers concerned for their baby's bones and teeth. Vivien buys a packet and she and Michelle nibble at a piece each when no one else is around.

When Michelle was four and a half, Andrew was walking with her in Gravesend, Kent, when two men dressed as reindeer leapt out of the door of the post office.

'We're promoting the new Christmas stamps,' one of them said. 'Would your little girl like to appear in a photograph with us?'

The following week the newspapers contained a picture of Michelle with the stamps and a not-very-convincing reindeer on each side of her.

Like many children, Michelle has always had a habit of running everywhere. Whenever there was an accident waiting to happen Michelle would head straight for it at lightning speed.

She and Simon went to stay at their grandparents' house once. Within five minutes of arriving Michelle had run and fallen over one of the chairs. Her tooth went right through her lower lip and she ended up going to hospital to have stitches put in. Simon just saw the funny side of it all.

She has always loved exploring the dressing-up box and would emerge looking like a queen or princess. Then she would run around proudly outside and fall in a mud puddle or trip over something.

One time Andrew waited outside Michelle's school as the children emerged. He watched as prettily clad little girls skipped to their parents and neat little boys dashed to play yet another game of chase. Then Michelle emerged, covered from head to foot in mud. Her new coat, clean on that morning, was almost unrecognizable.

'Hi, Dad,' she said cheerfully.

Meanwhile, in 1988, Andrew had joined the Essex Police Force and life seemed to get better and better. He had considered joining the police once before. Now he saw it as a way of helping society and a means of getting the security, pension and salary he wanted.

He wondered if he would pass the fitness test. A few months previously he had been in a motorbike accident and had ended up with a smashed right knee. In the end, he was accepted despite his condition.

It seemed an exciting job with all kinds of possibilities. After training college he started on foot patrol, then began working in a patrol car. He loved the sense of adventure—anything could happen.

One evening he was out on patrol in a car and coming towards the end of his shift. As he drove along he spotted a yellow van and recalled having heard something said about a yellow van earlier on. He stopped the van and had a chat with the driver.

The driver seemed quite reasonable. So did his lady passenger. After running checks on the van Andrew and his colleague decided to detain the couple for further questioning. There was a suspicion about some stolen cheques from Suffolk.

Andrew said to the man: 'Look, if there's no problem you'll be released quite soon. Don't worry.'

Back at the station he phoned the Suffolk police and gave them some further details.

'I think we've got a murder investigation on our hands,' the officer at the other end of the line said half an hour later. 'Those cheques belonged to a man who recently went missing.'

As a result, the man and woman later went on trial for murder and were convicted and imprisoned. Andrew got a Chief Constable's commendation for his handling of the incident. What occurred to Andrew, though, was that the murderer had killed his victim by hitting him over the head with a hammer. And that same man had sat immediately behind Andrew in the patrol car all the way back to the police station!

Shortly after that, Andrew developed an interest in surveillance and criminal investigation. He had various periods of attachment to the Criminal Investigation Branch and thoroughly enjoyed it, even the more gruesome elements.

What he found particularly difficult, because of his own experience as a father, was attending the scene of cot deaths.

The first one he attended was that of a baby boy. He was able to detach his emotions to some extent because it was a boy.

'I know what you're going through,' he said to the bereaved mother. 'The same thing's happened to me.'

Later he got a letter of thanks from the parents.

The second cot death he had to deal with was that of a girl. This time he just couldn't face going into the sealed-off room. Fortunately, his sergeant was sympathetic and he was sent back to the station to work on something else.

Andrew could deal with all kinds of tragedies—suicides, road traffic accidents, even murders—but because of his personal experience, he would always find cot deaths the most difficult.

With a settled career and a growing family of two children and another on the way, Andrew and Vivien were enjoying life. Yet they were blissfully unaware that their bubble of joy was about to burst.

Vivien recalls:
It was raining hard on that mid-December day in 1989, as my husband Andrew drove into the car park at Colchester Hospital. The windscreen wipers beat their rhythmic tune as the rain hit the windscreen at an ever-increasing speed. The car park was full as usual. We searched the small, inadequate parking area for a space, but to no avail.

'Drop me at the main entrance and meet me in the waiting room,' I said. 'I don't suppose for one minute I'll be seen on time.'

Andrew drove the car towards the grim, grey building. The battered, dark-stained front doors stood open to those who dared enter the labyrinth of the seemingly endless Victorian corridors within.

That morning I had an appointment to see Dr Daniel Rivers on the gynaecology ward. I was eight weeks pregnant and had been referred there by my family doctor because of a brown discharge I was getting.

Andrew stopped the car and I quickly got out, hurrying the few steps towards the doors and out of the rain. I watched as Andrew turned the car around and drove out of the car park onto the main road to find a parking space in one of the side roads, a short distance away. I quickly turned and made my way to the reception area.

A friendly, middle-aged receptionist greeted me with a smile. After I had introduced myself she thrust a form across the desk and said: 'Take a seat and fill in this form. When you've finished bring it back to me.'

I took the form and walked to an empty seat. Sitting down, I began to fill in the form she had given me. As usual the waiting room was full—mothers with young children, expectant mothers, all waiting to be seen. As I had guessed, the doctors were behind schedule and no one was being seen on time. It looked as if I was going to be in for a long wait.

As I sat there completing the form I felt a tap on my shoulder. It was Andrew, dripping from head to toe. 'Rain hasn't stopped, then?' I said with a smile.

'I sat in the car for a bit hoping it would ease, but I'd have been there all day,' he said with a grimace. 'We'll have to invest in an umbrella.'

A pool of water began to accumulate on the floor around his feet.

With the form duly completed I got up and gave it to the receptionist.

'Take a seat and you'll be called soon,' she said.

Eventually, after about an hour, I was called in to see Dr Rivers. He was a short, portly man with receding black hair. I tend to compare ordinary folk with famous people I've seen in films or on TV. It's my way of remembering what they look like. The only way I could describe Dr Rivers is as a Danny DeVito lookalike—the smaller of the two stars in the film *Twins*.

After giving Dr Rivers the letter from my own doctor, I explained to him about the brown discharge I was getting. He did a brief examination and decided that, as I had a previous history of miscarriages, he would admit me to the ward for rest, observation and an ultrasonic scan. Andrew helped me get my things together and, once I was settled into bed, he went back home to the children.

I enjoyed a comfortable night on the ward with complete bedrest. The following morning Dr Rivers and a nurse wheeled in a mobile ultra-sonic scanner. They pulled the curtains around the bed and Dr Rivers angled the small monitor towards me so that I could see the picture. The small monitor blinked into life. Dr Rivers made a couple of small adjustments to the picture, then said to me: 'Lift your gown up over your stomach.'

He began to scan across my abdomen, using a small scanning head that he had covered in a clear, gel-like substance. The small screen showed a mass of indistinguishable white dots on a black background. It looked to me like a cluttered star field.

Dr Rivers gazed intently at the screen, occasionally turning a knob to make yet another adjustment to the picture. After what seemed like half an hour but was in reality probably only a few minutes, Dr Rivers turned to me.

'Mrs Fowle, I'm sorry, but the sac is empty. It appears the embryo has disintegrated. This sometimes happens in early pregnancy. The reasons aren't always clear. The important thing now is to minimize the risk of infection and carry out a D & C to evacuate the womb and clean it of any debris left behind.'

I was shocked at what I was hearing. The time-honoured but now controversial D & C (dilatation and curettage), or scrape, would remove the lining of the uterus, including any developing embryo. It might stop the infection but it would certainly kill my baby.

'But I still *feel* pregnant,' I said. 'I don't care what the scan shows; I'm not having a scrape. If my baby's gone, then I'd rather it went on its own.'

'Mrs Fowle, I think you're being silly. The scan shows quite clearly that the embryo has disintegrated for reasons we don't know. It could be weeks before you abort it naturally. It's for this reason—and the threat to your health should you develop an infection—that I recommend you have a D & C as soon as possible. May I suggest you have a think about it and I'll come by later and see you?'

Dr Rivers left the room. The nurse unplugged the scanner and began to wheel it away.

Just before she left the room I said to her: 'You probably think I'm being stupid, don't you? But as long as I feel pregnant I can't have the scrape. Call it mother's instinct if you like. I just can't go ahead with it.'

The nurse was very sympathetic. She stopped what she was doing, turned around and patted my hand gently. 'I understand,' she said simply. 'It'll come right in the end.'

I lay there thinking for a while, going over everything in my mind. Was I being silly by refusing to go ahead with the scrape? Was it just that my feelings were all mixed up? Was I wrong to feel this way? No, I knew how I felt; the scan was wrong.

From that moment on the fight for my baby's life had begun.

Later on that day the ward sister spoke to me.

'Dr Rivers has just called. He said you can go home and have a think about what he said earlier. If you decide to go ahead with the D & C in the next few days, then call and we'll make arrangements for you to come in. If not, and it doesn't come away naturally in the next four weeks, then see your family doctor and he'll refer you back here for a D & C.'

I agreed to this and was discharged the same day.

The next four weeks passed quickly. Christmas came and went, then New Year 1990. I must admit that with the threat of a miscarriage I didn't feel much like celebrating. But time moves on. Soon the four weeks were up, and I felt no different. In fact, the discharge had stopped and I felt even more pregnant than I had before.

I went to my doctor and explained the situation to him. He booked me in for another scan the same week.

The day of the scan arrived. Andrew drove me to the hospital as before. It was a cold, sunny January day, the frost from the previous night gradually succumbing to the warmth of the sun. After parking the car in one of the side roads near the hospital, we walked together towards the big, grey building that somehow didn't seem so daunting in the bright sunshine. Part of me feared what the ultra-sound scan might soon reveal. Another part of me somehow knew it was going to be a great day.

No one was more surprised than Dr Rivers when the picture on the scanner's monitor showed a healthy twelve-week-old foetus. The doctor was lost for words. I can't begin to imagine what he must have felt. I on the other hand was elated that my instincts were right.

The next six months passed quickly with no undue worries. The doctors decided that the baby, like my previous three, would be born by Caesarean section. So at 9.30am on 23 July 1990, in Colchester Maternity Hospital, Ashley Michael Charles Vivian was born, weighing in at 6lb 7oz (2.95 kg). Andrew, Simon, Michelle and I were so proud. Ashley's fight for life was won.

After Ashley's birth I remained in hospital for another ten days before I was allowed to take him home. Although he was born four weeks premature, Ashley was perfect. There were no major problems apart from an extra finger on one of his hands and the need for minor corrective surgery for an undescended testicle. We proudly took him home, showing him off to relatives and friends who visited to see the new arrival in the family.

During the next few weeks I watched as Ashley grew and developed. When he was about five weeks old, however, I noticed that his eyes occasionally looked vacant and staring. It worried me. I'd move my finger across from one side to the other and he'd just stare straight ahead.

'He's blind!' I thought in panic. Andrew laughed and comforted me. Since Elizabeth's tragic death I was often worried about the children's health. It was only natural.

Another thing I noticed was that Ashley's head stayed floppy and needed support just as if he were still a newborn baby. When I talked to Andrew about it we booked to see our local doctor.

'I'm sure there's nothing to worry about here,' he assured us. The vacant staring was known as 'sunset eyes'. As for the floppiness, all children developed at different rates. Maybe he was just a late developer.

Over the next week or so, as with our other children at that age, I tried to get Ashley to smile, but he wouldn't. I knew instinctively then that something was wrong.

When the health visitor came, I talked things over with her. She examined him and found that Ashley's head was growing at an abnormal rate. His fontanel was hard and protruding. This diamond-shaped area found on top of all young babies' heads is normally soft because the bones in the baby's head haven't yet fused together. The hard protrusion suggested that there was pressure inside Ashley's head.

We took him first to Colchester General Hospital. After a check-up they sent us immediately to the Queen Elizabeth Children's Hospital in Hackney, London.

It was a busy time for us. After examining Ashley there, the doctors sent him for a scan at Great Ormond Street Hospital for Sick Children in London. The CAT (computerized axial tomography), now better known as the CT scan, uses a computer to arrange a series of X-ray images to show up soft tissues not normally seen in conventional X-rays.

Back at Queen Elizabeth Children's Hospital we were given some news that devastated us. Ashley had been diagnosed with a condition called hydrocephalus, popularly known as 'water on the brain'.

For some reason the cerebrospinal fluid in his brain wasn't being absorbed into the rest of his body. If left untreated, his head would gradually swell up until the pressure killed him.

I had a mixture of feelings all whirling around in my mind. First there was Elizabeth's tragic death, then the scare about Michelle. Now Ashley had this terrible problem that could lead to his death.

Like Andrew, I felt devastated. But I also felt as if I was suspended in mid-air, with no control over what was happening or which direction I should turn. I was helpless, unable to say or do anything constructive to help my little son, Ashley.

Oh, how I wished it was me and not him!

4 Shrunk in the Wash

'Years ago hydrocephalus was always fatal,' Miss Jane Blanchard, the specialist at Queen Elizabeth Children's Hospital, London, told Andrew and Vivien. 'But with today's technology it can be controlled with a minor operation to insert a tube known as a shunt.'

She explained that between the surface of Ashley's brain and the protective skull there were three layers of membranes called the *meninges*. In the gap within two of these layers was a water-based liquid known as *cerebrospinal fluid*. This was produced by special cells in the four hollow spaces in the brain, the *ventricles*. The fluid in Ashley's brain acted as a cushion against blows for the delicate structures of his brain. It also brought nutrients from the blood to Ashley's brain and carried waste products away from it.

'Even in a small baby like Ashley, the skull's fairly rigid,' she said. 'Any increase in the volume of cerebrospinal fluid causes pressure on the brain itself. And because the fluid in Ashley's brain can't escape easily, pressure is building up inside his head.'

Vivien shuddered at the thought of her precious little boy having suffered so many severe headaches in his short life because of this fluid pressing against his brain.

Miss Blanchard then produced a long, thin plastic tube. 'This is what a shunt looks like,' she said. 'We'll insert it into the ventricles of Ashley's brain through a small hole in the side of his skull, just above his ear. It works a bit like a drainpipe, carrying excess fluid away from the brain to the abdominal cavity. We'll attach a valve under the skin outside the entrance to his skull. This is to stop fluid going the wrong way back into his skull. To do this part of the operation I'll have to cut a flap of skin one centimetre across.'

'This part?' Andrew asked, wondering how much more there was to tell. 'What else is involved in this operation?'

'Well, we'll insert the tube down the side of Ashley's neck inside his skin right into his body cavity. I'll have to make a second small incision in Ashley's tummy so that the shunt tubing can be zigzagged inside him. That'll mean that as he grows the shunt will grow with him.'

Miss Blanchard handed them a whole pile of literature explaining the procedure. Left to itself, hydrocephalus could result in brain damage. Ashley's head would slowly get bigger and bigger until the pressure inside became so great that he would almost certainly die a slow, agonizing death. He was already having a lot of pain which Vivien presumed resulted from severe headaches. They knew the pain would get much worse as time went on.

'That's why Ashley's operation is so crucial,' Miss Blanchard concluded.

Andrew and Vivien decided straight away to go ahead with the operation. They couldn't face letting his suffering get any worse. In any case, the operation wouldn't show much afterwards. There would be a small scar on Ashley's scalp, but this would be covered after his hair grew back. There would be a slight bump at the point where the shunt entered his skull. There would also be a scar on his abdomen, similar to that left after an operation to remove the appendix.

The operation was carried out by Miss Blanchard at Queen Elizabeth Hospital in October 1990, when Ashley was ten weeks old. It lasted just under two hours.

Although it was a fairly routine operation, there is always a greater risk in operating on the brain than with other operations. Vivien in particular was worried. When at last Ashley came out of the operating theatre Andrew and Vivien were both very relieved.

A few days later they took Ashley home, confident that he was now on the mend. They had been assured that the shunt would make him better, but it seemed to have little effect. Gradually over the coming weeks his pain seemed to become worse rather than better. Ashley spent much of his time crying, and he was constantly sick. He just couldn't keep his milk down.

Their family doctor prescribed him an anti-sickness drug, but it didn't improve things very much. Christmas 1990 came and went. The doctor tried another drug to calm down the sickness. This worked for a time but soon little Ashley was crying with the pain and finding it difficult to keep down his milk again.

In February the three of them, Andrew, Vivien and baby Ashley, went to York for a long weekend. Simon and Michelle went to stay with their grandparents. But what was supposed to be a pleasant time away from the routine of things turned into disaster. Ashley spent much of the time screaming with pain. Andrew phoned the hospital from York and told Miss Blanchard what was happening.

'Bring him down to the hospital straight away,' she said to them, a sense of urgency in her voice.

They drove from York all the way to the Queen Elizabeth Hospital in London. Ashley, now seven months old, was once again sent to Great Ormond Street Hospital for a CT scan. This confirmed that the pressure in his head was building up. The shunt didn't seem to be working. Andrew and Vivien had been warned that something like this could happen at any time in the future if the shunt got blocked, but it seemed so soon after the operation.

Ashley was admitted back into hospital and had to have another operation. During it they replaced the whole shunt. It turned out that the original shunt hadn't worked at all because of a manufacturing fault. The only way the pressure on Ashley's brain had been relieved was by the fluid forcing its way out along the narrow gap between the shunt and the skull. Then the fluid had filtered its way down under Ashley's skin and been dispersed.

Andrew and Vivien had often noticed a balloon of skin around the opening of the shunt but had not realized its significance. No wonder Ashley had been so uncomfortable.

The new shunt made a dramatic difference. At last Ashley was free of the pain of headaches. He slept peacefully between feeds and he no longer needed the anti-sickness drugs. Apart from a minor problem with tonsillitis in May, everything had settled back into the normal routine.

After Ashley had been diagnosed with hydrocephalus Vivien's sister Jackie had come to them with an unusual confession.

'I don't know how you're going to take this, Viv, but before Ashley was born I was told that you were going to have a boy,' she said. 'He was going to be very ill during his life, but he wouldn't die.'

'Who told you that?' demanded Vivien, shocked at what she heard.

'I don't know, really. I suppose, looking back, it was God. You may think I'm being silly, but I told my husband about it at the time, if you don't believe me. I think this hydrocephalus is the illness I was told about.'

Jackie's words gave Andrew and Vivien a hope to cling to during the difficult months that followed. At least Ashley wasn't going to die.

In October 1991 Andrew transferred from the Essex police force to Kent. The family moved to the Kentish village of Hunton. A couple of times while they lived in Hunton Ashley developed virus infections around the site of the shunt and had to be taken to Maidstone General Hospital for treatment.

During the time they were in Hunton Ashley also had a number of breath-holding fits. When he got into a temper he would hold his breath until he went blue. His eyes would then glaze over and he would pass out. Once he had fainted he would automatically start breathing again, so there was no risk of serious injury. Remembering Elizabeth's tragic death, Vivien in particular became very worried. The more worried she became, the more Ashley seemed to hold his breath.

In December 1991 their local doctor prescribed Ashley an anti-convulsant drug to prevent fits. He took this for the next year. The doctors weren't very worried about him. The problem was quite common in small children and they said it was almost certainly attention-seeking when Ashley was angry. They recommended that Andrew and Vivien ignore the fits, which they did. Gradually he stopped having fits because they were no longer having the desired effect on his parents.

February 1992 came. Once again Ashley started crying for no apparent reason and getting what seemed to be headaches. He also broke out into cold, clammy sweats. Once more they phoned Queen Elizabeth Children's Hospital to say that something wasn't right with his shunt.

This time the doctors there took him into the hospital for observation. Once again Simon and Michelle had to manage without their parents and little brother being around. As with any young children, they felt disturbed when they were away from their parents for any length of time. But they were getting used to it. Thankfully, they had their grandparents to look after them and help them to have at least some semblance of a normal life.

At the hospital, the doctors put a needle into the shunt through Ashley's skin. They connected this to a special gauge that measured the pressure of the cerebrospinal fluid using a mercury scale similar to the one used in testing blood pressure. After this, Ashley had another CT scan. The doctors concluded that the shunt wasn't working because of a blockage in the valve. This time, instead of the full-scale operation, they did what was termed a shunt revision, replacing the valve.

Soon eighteen-month-old Ashley was back home, none the worse for his ordeal. Operations were becoming almost routine in his life.

By now he was gradually learning to walk. It seemed to take months for him to take a few more steps. Andrew and Vivien were surprised how long it took him compared with Simon and Michelle. They also noticed how unco-ordinated his walking was. His legs were bent and spread wide apart and he fell over a lot. He also had weak arms.

The doctors at Queen Elizabeth Children's Hospital checked his walking and diagnosed him as having a condition known as Dandy-Walker Syndrome after Dr Walter Dandy (1886-1946) and Dr Arthur Walker (born 1907). The name could equally have come from the earliest form of bicycles: a flamboyantly-dressed gentleman (known as a 'dandy') would sit astride a hobby-horse on wheels and use his feet to kick the ground and propel himself along. Inevitably, the bike was given the name 'dandy-horse' and the leg movement was called 'dandy-walking'.

In addition, Ashley had ataxic gait, which meant simply that he was unable to co-ordinate his walking.

These two conditions resulted from problems in the balance part of his brain. The doctors concluded that they were a side effect of his hydrocephalus. They prescribed regular physiotherapy to get Ashley's limbs working better and they agreed to see him regularly.

Once more life returned to normal. Andrew and Vivien learned to live with Ashley's illness and its associated disabilities. In August 1992 they bought their own terraced house in Northfleet, Kent. They were determined to move as quickly as possible because in Hunton they had been burgled.

Soon after the move, two-year-old Ashley started nursery school. His regular physiotherapy was doing him good. He was walking well and beginning to catch up with other children of his age.

Ashley then came under the care of Dr David Leung, a paediatrician at the Livingstone Child Development Centre in Dartford, Kent. Over the following months he watched as Ashley began to walk much better and to talk fluently. He seemed to be more than making up for the setbacks he had encountered during his short life.

Now that Ashley was moving around a lot more, he was taking more tumbles. All young children fall over regularly, but with Ashley's balance problems he was falling over many times a day. Dr Leung was concerned that if he fell and banged his head badly, this could make the hydrocephalus even worse. As a result, he sent Ashley to West Hill Hospital, also in Dartford, where they measured him up and fitted him out with a special helmet made of blue plastic material and lined with foam.

Ashley wore his helmet around the house and when he went out with his family. The helmet protected the sides and back of his head. It had openings for his ears, his face and the top of his head, and his blond hair stuck out of the top like fibres on a coconut. It was an unusual helmet but it soon became part of his way of life.

The rest of the family thought Ashley was cute in his helmet. Sometimes they thought he looked like a little Gladiator. That suited Ashley. 'Gladiators' was his favourite TV show. At other times they could imagine him sitting on a miniature motorbike, wearing his protective headgear. Simon and Michelle loved to sneak up on Ashley and knock gently on his helmet, then disappear before he had time to look round. Then the three of them would squeal with delight and Simon and Michelle would start all over again.

One time they went to a park surrounding New Tavern Fort, next to the promenade in Gravesend. Ashley took off his helmet and sat for some photographs on a 2,000lb bomb dropped by the Germans in the Second World War. That very bomb had landed in the back garden of a house in Mitchell Avenue, Northfleet, which later became the home of Vivien's parents. When Charlie and Ann first moved there they noticed a dip in the garden. It was only much later that they found out that the dip was the result of the crater made by the bomb and the digging needed to get it out.

One evening in November 1993 a leaflet came through Andrew and Vivien's door from a church down the road. It advertised a 'miracle and healing' meeting at Earls Court in London, led by an evangelist called Morris Cerullo.

Although she no longer went to church, Vivien wanted to go to this meeting and take Ashley with her. 'Ashley could be healed!' she said excitedly.

Andrew was sceptical at first. But after thinking about it for a time he decided to speak with Mark Hayton, his sergeant at work, whose brother was a church pastor. After making some enquiries, the sergeant recommended that they go along. After all, it couldn't do any harm—and it might do a lot of good.

Earls Court arena was packed with thousands of people that night. Andrew and Vivien sat at the back, with Ashley on their laps. With a crescendo of organ music and rapturous applause, the short, balding figure of Morris Cerullo appeared on the stage. Soon there was a lot of exuberant singing, with people dancing in the aisles. It was all very noisy and disturbing for Ashley.

'I must admit, I felt nothing,' said Andrew later. 'I tried to pray along with all the other people, but I felt empty inside. It seemed as if God wasn't there.

'Towards the end of the meeting I got up to go to the toilet, leaving Vivien and Ashley in their seats. When I came back I found a young Chinese man standing over Ashley, who was seated on Vivien's lap. The man had put his hand on Ashley's head and was praying for him.

'For some reason Ashley had fallen asleep. That was strange. Ashley had been so restless through all the rest of the meeting. It seemed as if whatever was happening now was making him peaceful.

'I stood watching until the young man had finished praying. Then he stood up and introduced himself to us. He said his name was Paul Ki Ho Song. He told us he had wanted to pray for our little boy because he believed there was something wrong with his head.

'I was flabbergasted. We'd never met this man before in our lives. We didn't know him from Adam, yet in-stinctively he knew there was something wrong with Ashley. It wasn't as if you could *see* anything wrong with him. Without his distinctive helmet, which he only wore when he was playing, Ashley looked like any other child. It was only when he walked that people could tell he had some sort of disability—and he certainly hadn't walked while we were at Earls Court. There were just too many people about.

'There was only one conclusion I could come to. This man had been sent by God to pray for our son. I knew something was going to happen.

'Back at home Ashley's walking began to improve almost straight away. He became more steady on his feet and was less likely to fall over. We decided to try Ashley without the padded helmet he wore around the house every day.

'That suited Vivien just fine. For weeks she had tried sponging it clean, but that just didn't seem to have any effect. By now the smell of sweat and greasy hair had made the helmet disgusting, to say the least. Without any washing instructions to go by she stuck it in the automatic washing machine. When it came out it had shrunk.

'My dad took it, saying there was an old-fashioned hat shop in Frinton and maybe they could put it on one of their stretchers overnight. But when they took it off the next morning it shrank back into its original shape.

'We decided it would never again go back on Ashley's head. Vivien was delighted—she had always hated the thing. Ashley put it on one of his teddy bears and for months he cuddled it in bed with him whenever he went to stay at my parents' house.'

Considering the level of his continued disabilities, Ashley was now coping better and better. He was able to walk around the house and garden, and he could climb up and down the stairs. He was still using nappies at this stage, and he was unable to help his parents when they washed and dressed him. But, apart from that, things were looking better every day.

Andrew and Vivien were pleased with Ashley's progress. But the doctors were worried about some aspects of his development. Ashley was having trouble raising his arms above his shoulders. His muscles seemed to be wasting away around the area of his back and shoulders.

Dr David Leung at the Livingstone Hospital became concerned. He also believed that Ashley was developing a curved spine. As a result, he referred Ashley to Mr Morley at Guy's Hospital, London. A whole era of new difficulties for Ashley was about to begin.

5 A Testing Time

The appointment with Mr Morley took ages to come through. Andrew and Vivien were busy over the Christmas period and didn't give it a lot of thought. With three children all needing their attention they had more than enough to worry about apart quite from yet another routine appointment.

Eventually a time was made for Ashley, now three and a half years old, to see Mr Morley at the Newcomen Centre at Guy's Hospital, London, on Thursday, 24 February 1994.

The day of the appointment arrived. It was very much like any other day as they took the train to London. Little did they realize that their lives would never be quite the same again.

The Newcomen Centre greeted Andrew, Vivien and Ashley like a breath of fresh air. Its modern exterior contrasted sharply with the decaying Victorian children's hospital that stood next to it, a monument to the ideals of a grand, industrial age long since past.

They walked through the automatic doors to the reception area, where they introduced themselves. The receptionist asked if Ashley had been to the X-ray department. He hadn't, so they were given a small slip of paper and told to take him to the main building for a back X-ray.

After a walk through the corridors they sat and waited while Ashley had his 'pictures taken', as he liked to call it. Soon they were handed a big, brown envelope with the finished X-rays in it. Back in the Newcomen Centre they handed this to the receptionist and were told to take a seat in the waiting room.

Space to sit down was limited. Much of the fitted seating was taken up with children's toys. Eventually, Andrew and Vivien managed to find a space and they squeezed their way into the corner. Then they sat and watched as Ashley amused himself with the toy cars.

There were several other parents waiting, their children with various disabilities. Gradually, parents left with their children as their names were called out. At last it was Ashley's turn.

They were shown into a large room at the end of a long corridor. It was sparsely furnished with white walls—typical of the many medical rooms they had been in with Ashley during his short life.

As they walked through the door they were greeted by five people who sat at the opposite end of the room in a semi-circle facing them. Andrew and Vivien were introduced to the people they hadn't met before. There was Mr Morley, the orthopaedic specialist; Professor James Richardson, the neurologist; another doctor whom they knew simply as Dr Robb; Ashley's physiotherapist, Claire; and a secretary who would take notes.

Mr Morley studied Ashley's medical notes, then looked at the X-rays to see what was causing the muscle wasting in Ashley's neck and the curvature of his spine. The doctors watched as Ashley walked around the room. They tried out his reflexes and Mr Morley plied Andrew and Vivien with a host of questions about how Ashley was at home with his walking and other movements.

'Thank you, mother and father,' Mr Morley said formally to Andrew and Vivien after he had finished all his questioning. 'From what you've said and what I've seen here on these X-rays, I think this is more Professor Richardson's department. So I'm now handing Ashley's case over to him.'

Although he spoke in a voice lacking in emotion, Andrew and Vivien guessed that something serious was up. Professor Richardson was, after all, a specialist in problems to do with the brain and spinal cord.

Professor Richardson took the notes and glanced down at them. 'Hmm,' he said at last. 'I think we need a bit more information about what's going on in Ashley's nervous system. I recommend that Ashley has an MRI (magnetic resonance imaging) scan of his upper spine and lower brain stem. It doesn't hurt, but it'll give us a lot more to go on. We can admit him over the weekend and do the scan on Monday. What do you think?'

'We're in your hands, sir,' said Andrew, politely. Deep inside he was shaking with fear at what could be wrong with his son. 'If that helps you get to the bottom of Ashley's problem, you have our permission.'

'OK, see you next week, then.'

The following Sunday they took Ashley to Guy's Hospital in London, where he was admitted to Ronnie MacKeith ward in The Tower, an extension of the hospital. The next day he had his scan.

MRI was a process that used a very powerful electromagnet linked to a computer to build up a series of cross-sectional images of the brain and spinal cord. These images were later transferred to film. It was a relatively new but highly safe way of examining Ashley's nervous system. Unlike the CT scans that Ashley had had as a baby, the MRI scan didn't use X-rays so there was no risk of radiation and no known side effects. It could also 'see through' the bones of the skull to the soft tissue underneath.

Ashley was first given a mild general anaesthetic so that he wouldn't be frightened or accidentally move while the scan was being done. A special dye was injected into him to show up the nerve cells more clearly. He was then laid on a couch inside a tunnel-shaped metal cylinder open at both ends. The cylinder was in fact a large electromagnet.

Magnetic currents were used to magnetize hydrogen atoms in Ashley's body. Signals from these were picked up by radio waves and processed by a computer. A series of 'slices' through Ashley's brain and spinal cord was produced. Later these would be printed out onto black-and-white film in much the same way as X-rays are produced. An MRI scan showed the details much more clearly than a CT scan, but the whole process took considerably longer—Ashley was in the tunnel for about an hour and a half.

On Tuesday, the day after the scan, Ashley was allowed home to give him time to recover from the general anaesthetic before the next step was decided.

Three days later he was back in Guy's Hospital. Andrew and Vivien were getting weary from the stress and hassle of all these trips to different hospitals in London. From Guy's, Ashley was sent by ambulance to St Thomas's Hospital for yet another form of scan, a PET scan.

PET (positron emission tomography) was an even newer and more sophisticated scanning process than MRI. Like MRI it took a series of cross-sectional pictures of the body that were fed into a computer. Unlike MRI, which produced pictures in black and white, Ashley's PET images were converted by a computer into a detailed picture complete with colour-enhanced views of the hot and cold spots in Ashley's brain and spinal cord. It was the same technology used to take colour-enhanced pictures of the earth from space to show hot and cold areas.

Ashley returned to Guy's Hospital and a couple of days later Andrew and Vivien had a meeting with Professor Richardson.

'I've looked at Ashley's MRI scan and clearly there's something that shouldn't be there,' he began.

'What do you mean?' asked Andrew, concern in his voice.

'I think we're looking at some kind of growth that's pushing on Ashley's brain and spine. That's why he's having difficulties standing up straight and walking.'

'Growth? What kind of growth?' Panic was almost choking Andrew as he spoke.

'I think we're looking at a tumour here. It seems to be a fairly large tumour that runs from the spinal cord up into the brain stem. Now, I was hoping the PET scan would show us a bit more. All I can tell from it, though, is that the tumour has a slow metabolism.'

'What's that?' asked Vivien, still not able to take in the fact that this doctor had said her son had a tumour.

'Metabolism simply refers to the rate of growth. If a tumour has a fast metabolism—in other words, if it's growing quickly—that's much more worrying than one with a slow metabolism.'

'What happens next?' asked Andrew.

'Let's meet again on Tuesday and I'll invite my colleague, Dr Audrey. Together we should be able to get to the bottom of things.'

The following Tuesday, 8 March, while Ashley played with the other children on the ward, Andrew and Vivien met Dr Paul Audrey for the first time. He was an intellectual-looking doctor, dressed in an old-fashioned way with round 'John Lennon' glasses. Vivien thought he looked like a cross between Glenn Miller and Buddy Holly.

Professor Richardson summarized things so far, then handed over the meeting to Dr Audrey.

'Yes, well, I propose doing a biopsy on young Ashley,' Dr Audrey said in his plummy voice. 'A biopsy is an operation to remove a small piece of tissue for examining in the laboratory. In Ashley's case I would remove the tissue from the area around Ashley's brain stem to find out the cause of his problems.'

'You mean a brain operation?' asked Vivien incredulously.

'In a manner of speaking, yes. Of course, we aren't talking here about a major brain operation. I would simply go through to the brain's surface and remove the small amount of tissue needed.'

'What sort of risk is involved?' asked Andrew.

'There's always a risk in any operation. This one is no more or less risky than any other. The decision, of course, is yours. We can go for a biopsy now, or leave it six months and do another MRI scan to see if there's any change. But if we leave it, we won't know what we're dealing with.'

'We're happy to be guided by you,' Andrew said.

By the end of the meeting they had agreed to Ashley having a biopsy. The operation would be delayed a month until the beginning of April 1994 because Dr Audrey had arranged to to go on leave and couldn't at that stage change his plans.

Back at home Andrew and Vivien, worried about Ashley's long-term future, began to read up as much as they could about tumours. The forthcoming biopsy, they realized, was to discover whether Ashley's tumour was benign or malignant. They just hoped and prayed it would be benign.

Benign brain tumours do not contain cancer cells. They have distinct borders and do not generally invade nearby tissue. A wart on a person's finger is a benign tumour. The difference between a benign tumour on the finger and one on the brain is that if the latter grows larger it might press on the surrounding nerve tissue, causing severe headaches or worse. Benign brain tumours are often removed by an operation. Tumours of the spinal cord are much more difficult to operate on.

Malignant brain tumours, on the other hand, contain cancer cells and are much more serious. If Ashley had one of those it could interfere with his body's functions and could even be life-threatening. Like a growing plant, it could put out roots into healthy tissue and the cancer would spread.

Cancer. The very word struck terror into Vivien's heart. Yet she discovered that cancer is now treatable by a range of different approaches.

She learned that cancer is not a single condition but a group of over 200 different diseases. What they have in common is that they affect the tiny building blocks known as cells that make up a person's organs and tissues. Normal healthy cells reproduce themselves by dividing in a controlled and orderly manner. If for some reason this process gets out of control, a lump develops, which is known as a tumour.

Sometimes, cells break away from this primary tumour and travel to other parts of the body through the blood or lymph system. There they form another, secondary, tumour. Many malignant brain tumours, Vivien found out, are formed in this way. If the brain tumour is a primary one, as it probably was in Ashley's case, it rarely spreads elsewhere.

In spring 1994 Andrew and Vivien felt drawn towards going to church again. They had heard about Gravesend Christian Fellowship and went along as a family to a Sunday meeting. The church had been formed as a kind of 'daughter church' by Dartford Christian Fellowship. It had first started as a weekly meeting in someone's home, but by April 1992 it had become a full church with thirty adult members. Nearly two years later the church had grown to fifty adult members and forty children.

At the end of one meeting, Andrew talked with the church's pastor, Dave Webster, about how he had given up on God over his daughter's death.

'One thing I'm worried about,' said Andrew. 'If I come back to God, is it just because I'm concerned about Ashley, or is it for pure motives?'

They had an intense discussion. As a result, both Andrew and Vivien decided to join the church and go through a series of classes to learn more about what commitment to church membership meant.

The following Saturday night, things at home took a sudden turn for the worse. Andrew was looking into Ashley's eyes when he noticed something he had never seen before. Ashley's eyes seemed odd. The pupil in one eye was big while the pupil in the other was small. Something serious was wrong.

'What happens if he dies?' thought Andrew, remembering what little Elizabeth's eyes had looked like in death. *'God, please help us.'*

6 Sweet Sleep

Andrew decided to phone the Maudsley Hospital in London, telling them about Ashley's eyes.

'Get him here first thing tomorrow morning,' the nursing sister said, trying her best not to show concern in her voice.

Fortunately, getting to the hospital so early on a Sunday morning was no great problem. In the short time they had been going to Gravesend Christian Fellowship they had got to know Gill Smith, a woman who was deeply concerned for Ashley. She had agreed to pray regularly for him and had offered to help Andrew and Vivien with a ride in her car whenever they needed it. Now was a time when they really needed her help.

Andrew rang her up.

'Hi, Gill, it's Andrew Fowle here. I'm sorry if I've got you out of bed so early.'

'No, I was up already. How's Ashley?'

'Not too good, I'm afraid. Last night I looked into his eyes and noticed that his pupils were different sizes. The Maudsley Hospital want to admit him right away.'

'I'm sorry to hear that. Do you want me to run you up to the hospital?'

'Yes, please. If it isn't too much trouble.'

'No, of course it isn't. I'd be delighted to help. See you in a few minutes.'

Soon they were on their way, dropping off Simon and Michelle at the home of Vivien's parents. Traffic in London at that time on a Sunday morning is usually very light and they got to the hospital in good time. Looking at her watch, Gill reckoned that she would even be able to get back in time for the morning meeting at their church.

Once the doctors had seen Ashley, they decided to admit him into hospital straight away. Andrew and Vivien planned to stay at the hospital while Simon and Michelle were looked after by their grandparents.

The doctor noted in the records: *'Ashley has poor head control, unsteady gait, cannot run and is unable to raise his arms above his head. He has a marked curvature of the spine. Mental development is normal, and he plays as a normal child of his age.'*

The reason for Ashley coming into hospital was, according to the notes, *'to receive steroid therapy to reduce the swelling (oedema) around the tumour caused by the build-up of fluid and to prepare for the biopsy of his tumour'*. Ashley said it was for the doctors and nurses 'to look at the bump on my head'.

Over the next twenty-four hours the doctors decided that Ashley's condition had deteriorated enough to warrant an urgent biopsy. They couldn't wait another three weeks until Dr Audrey got back from his holiday. They had to act *now*.

Another consultant neurosurgeon, Dr Graham Pollard, was chosen to carry out the operation. Although highly skilled, he operated mainly on adults rather than children. The operation was due to take place on Wednesday, 16 March. Andrew and Vivien had a meeting with him the day before.

To Vivien, Dr Pollard looked like Doc Brown from the film *Back to the Future*. He was casually dressed and wore old-fashioned glasses with thick, black frames.

Dr Pollard began by telling them a bit about Ashley's brain and spinal cord. 'Together they form his central nervous system,' he said. 'This controls Ashley's senses, emotions, thoughts and memory.

'The brain is soft and spongy and is made up of forty billion nerve cells as well as supportive tissue. There are three parts: the cerebrum with its right and left cerebral hemispheres, the cerebellum and the brain stem.

'The brain stem is the part we're interested in here. In Ashley it's not much bigger than your thumb but it's the part of the brain that controls his hunger and thirst as well as his basic body functions such as body temperature, blood pressure, swallowing and breathing.'

'All that?' said Andrew.

'Yes, it's amazing. Anyway, the brain stem joins onto Ashley's spinal cord. That's made up of bundles of nerve fibres and runs through a canal in the centre of the spine. Of course, the backbone protects the spinal cord. So does the cerebrospinal fluid that surrounds it.'

'So there's fluid in the spine as well?' asked Andrew. This was becoming more like a biology lesson.

'Yes, that's right. Now, this biopsy we're going to do involves opening up the base of Ashley's skull and removing a tiny piece of tumour from his brain stem. It's a very delicate operation. The important thing to realize is that, unlike other cells in the body, nerve cells don't reproduce themselves. That means we have to be very careful when we go in so we don't damage any of the nerve cells.'

Andrew, hopeful that the operation could be the beginning of solving Ashley's problem, chipped in with a question. 'If, once you get into Ashley's brain stem, you find you can remove more of the tumour than you thought, will you do it?'

'Well, yes, of course. I'll remove as much of the tumour as it's safe to remove,' he assured them.

A thrill of hope went through Andrew's whole being. Maybe, just maybe, this evil monster called a tumour could be cut out once and for all from little Ashley's brain stem.

Wednesday. The day of the operation had arrived. The hospital staff recorded that Ashley was in a lot of pain and very frightened that day. Andrew and Vivien were also very anxious and in need of support. The medical team wrote down their aims: 'To ensure Ashley is painfree using oral analgesia, careful positioning and distraction; explain all procedures to Ashley and his family; and encourage expression of fears and anxieties.'

Ashley's analgesic worked, and soon he was sedated, if not entirely happy. It was a relief to Andrew and Vivien to see him calm instead of crying out not to have to go through yet another operation.

In the operating theatre the nurses had difficulty finding a vein for Ashley's intravenous injection. He had had so many injections in his short life that the veins had become difficult to detect and penetrate. Eventually they managed to locate one in his foot and put a drip in there.

For the next two hours Andrew and Vivien had to sit waiting for news of how the operation had gone. They talked and tried to read, but it was difficult to concentrate. It was a long, slow morning. Meanwhile, the operation was progressing, carried out by neurosurgeon Dr Pollard and his team.

During the operation Ashley was anaesthetized and placed face down with his head resting on a horseshoe-shaped support. Ashley's hair at the back of his head was shaved. Dr Pollard cut a straight line through the skin down the back of Ashley's head. He then made a small hole into the lower part of Ashley's skull.

Using a microscope he opened the outer of the three meninges (the membrane known as the *dura*) covering the top of the spinal cord. There before him was the monster itself—the greyish-white area of the tumour. Carefully, he cut a couple of tiny samples and sent them for analysis. Then, after taking some photographs, he stitched Ashley's head up again.

Once Ashley had recovered consciousness, Dr Pollard came to tell Andrew and Vivien the news.

'The operation was a complete success,' he said. 'Everything went according to plan and Ashley will soon be out of the theatre.'

'What about the tumour?' asked Andrew, hope rising in him once again. 'Were you able to get rid of it?'

'No, I'm sorry. I was only able to remove just enough tissue for a biopsy. It was too dangerous even to attempt to remove any more.'

Their dreams of instant recovery were shattered. But at least Ashley was alive, and soon they would be able to see him.

Ashley recovered quite quickly from his operation. Within two days he was speaking well and swallowing.

The wound took over a week to settle down, though gradually it healed up.

Over the next few days, Andrew and Vivien stayed with Ashley as he recovered. They tried to explain to him what was going on—why he was here and why he had needed the operation. But he found it all so difficult to understand because he felt normal. How could he *possibly* have something in his head that shouldn't be there?

One nurse at the Maudsley was particularly helpful. Dee was short, with glasses and red cheeks to match her red hair. She fell in love with Ashley. She was always buying or making him things. She bought him Patch the Dog and a Thomas the Tank Engine jigsaw puzzle. She made him a treasured cuddly toy called Sydney Slapstick and bought him a special teddy that he called Burly Bear. Dee was bubbly and happy. She always tried to be more optimistic than the doctors.

Ashley took to Dee as much as she took to him. 'She was my favourite nurse 'cos she let me have my dinner with her,' he said once.

Gradually Vivien got to know some of the other parents and children on the ward.

There was Jason Males, an older boy who lived just five minutes down the road from Ashley's family. He was being discharged just as Ashley was being admitted. But at least they had met each other, though it was so far from home.

There was an older woman, Sylvia, whose grand-daughter Kaleigh had had a stroke when she was much younger. Now seven, Kaleigh had been brought in because she was having fits and was very unwell.

Vivien and Sylvia shared a room and got to know each other well. Sylvia was a Christian who talked a lot about God. She always had time for Vivien, and she was a great encourager. She also kept trying to get Andrew and Vivien to laugh.

If Sylvia hadn't been there it would have been a very miserable time for them both. It was a depressing place. The hospital was old and decrepit, and Vivien thought it was more like a 'nut house' than a place for sick children.

It took eight days for the results of the biopsy to come through. The piece of tumour had been examined under the microscope. The laboratory reported it to be a 'mixed ependymoma and astrocytoma WHO grade 2'. An astrocytoma is a tumour arising in the astrocyte cells, the star-like cells that form part of the brain's supportive tissue.

This meant that Ashley's tumour was a low-level malignant one. If it had been diagnosed grade 4 on the WHO scale it would have been highly malignant and much faster growing. At least that was some consolation.

Andrew and Vivien were devastated, but grateful at least to know that it wasn't the worst form of cancer. The impact of the news took a few minutes to sink in. As Vivien walked back to the ward from the meeting, she collapsed on the floor in the corridor. She woke up ten minutes later to find herself on a bed in the treatment room. The nightmare hadn't ended; her little son still had a malignant tumour.

On Friday, 25 March, ten days after the biopsy, Ashley was allowed to go home. Dr Pollard referred them back to Professor Richardson, and an appointment was made with him for the following Tuesday.

The fateful day came all too quickly and, in 'Death Row', Andrew and Vivien were told the devastating news that the brain-stem tumour Ashley had would almost certainly lead to his death within five years.

Chemotherapy and operating to remove the tumour were not options. That left radiotherapy as the last resort.

The prognosis wasn't at all good. Dr H.J.G. Bloom of the Royal Marsden Hospital, London, had reported that, of 415 patients under sixteen completing radiotherapy for all types of brain tumours between 1970 and 1980, 53 per cent survived five years. This declined to 45 per cent after ten years and 41 per cent after twenty years. According to American neurosurgeons writing in 1986, most children with brain-stem tumours like Ashley's died within just two years.

That afternoon Andrew and Vivien took Ashley home on the train in despair.

Andrew felt as if God had it in for them. 'He isn't happy just with taking one of our children,' Andrew thought. 'He wants Ashley as well. God, what would you achieve by taking Ashley away from us? It certainly wouldn't bring me any closer to you. In fact, it'd only serve to drive me further away from you. If you're punishing me, then take *me,* not my children.'

When Jackie, Vivien's sister, heard that Ashley had a malignant tumour she did everything she could to avoid seeing her little nephew. She had been nearby when her little niece, Elizabeth, had died in her cot. Now she couldn't stand the thought of Ashley dying as well. It was OK talking to Vivien on the phone, but Jackie avoided going around to her house. That way she could stay detached and wouldn't get emotionally involved.

Vivien, on the other hand, kept going over to see her sister and gradually Jackie came to believe that God had impressed on her to pray for Ashley. Sometimes she got up at four in the morning to pray for him. At the same time she couldn't bear looking at Ashley. She was almost frightened to get too close to him. It was an emotionally confusing time for her.

'I felt as if I was arguing with God,' recalled Jackie later. 'I kept asking him to find someone else and he seemed to say: "No, it's you who needs to help." '

The result was that Jackie asked Vivien if she would mind if two church members, Kevin Reilly and Gill Smith, who had taken them to hospital, could come and pray for Ashley.

Each time Kevin and Gill prayed with their hands on Ashley's head, he fell into a peaceful sleep. Andrew and Vivien thought all the parents of young children in the neighbourhood would ask Kevin and Gill to perform the same miracle on their overactive children, if only they knew!

Ashley might enjoy peaceful sleep without having to try. But sleep didn't come easily to Andrew and Vivien, as they waited anxiously for Ashley's radiotherapy to begin.

7 *Attack From Behind*

Andrew and Vivien's decision to go ahead with radiotherapy for Ashley following the fateful meeting on 29 March had been a big one. They knew there could be side-effects—sickness, nausea, even permanent damage to his backbone. They also had to face the fact that even with low-grade tumours, such as the one Ashley had, most of them eventually recurred after radiotherapy.

Following that meeting they had been in a quandary. If they left things, there would be a high risk that the tumour would grow and Ashley's condition deteriorate. The radiotherapy would seriously affect Ashley, yet they wanted to keep him alive as long as possible. Who knows? Perhaps one day a new form of chemotherapy, like the one they were told about, might be available to treat Ashley's condition.

Radiotherapy, it seemed, was their last chance to save their precious little son.

Dr Joan Whitehead, the consultant radiotherapist, wrote: 'After lengthy discussion with Ashley's parents, we agreed to proceed with irradiation. This was on the basis that although we feel that this tumour may not be cured, our main intent is to maintain as high a quality of life as possible for Ashley over the next few years. We anticipate that he will probably eventually have a further tumour progression.'

The MRI scan had shown a long tumour on Ashley's spinal cord. It extended from the neck region up into the brain stem itself. There was also a cyst from his neck downwards along the spinal cord. Something had to be done—and done fast.

Radiotherapy, Andrew and Vivien discovered, treated tumours by using high energy rays to bombard abnormal cells. They were assured that it wouldn't make Ashley radioactive and he wasn't a danger to other people while he was being treated.

The preparation for radiotherapy involved several visits to the hospital. Fortunately, Andrew and Vivien had the support of both sets of grandparents to look after Simon and Michelle while they were away. They had also made friends with Lee Rawlinson, a young man from the church who spent a lot of his free time with the Fowles. Now that the children had got to know him, Lee, together with his girlfriend Sharon, made the ideal babysitter for Simon and Michelle while their parents were at the hospital with Ashley. It was great to have the support of real friends.

On Sunday, 10 April, the hospital anaesthetized Ashley and made a special Perspex mask moulded exactly to the shape of his face. It was a very close fit and was solid except for simple air tubes from the nostrils so that Ashley could breathe while he was being given the radiation. There were two straight Perspex brackets, one on each side of the mask, so that his head could be clamped face down onto the table in exactly the right place.

A week later, again on Sunday, Ashley was back at the hospital. This time he was anaesthetized to have various positioning marks tattooed into his skin along the line of his backbone. This was to help the radiographer to direct the rays to the exact site. They were made in permanent ink because they had to remain visible for the whole six weeks while the treatment was taking place.

On the same day, Ashley's head was measured accurately and he was placed under a simulator. This took X-ray pictures of the area to be treated. The important thing was to direct the beams of radiation to the precise site of the tumour. If it strayed into other areas, even by a millimetre, it could damage some of the healthy brain and nerve tissue, with serious long-term effects.

That Sunday Andrew and Vivien also had an interview with Dr Joan Whitehead, who went over what they had previously discussed and answered their last-minute questions.

Ashley reluctantly co-operated with the preparation sessions, even though they weren't much fun. His parents sensed that, despite his young age, he somehow knew that the treatment he was about to start was vital.

Everything was now ready for the radiotherapy itself to begin in nine days' time. Andrew and Vivien decided that the whole family needed a break together before Ashley went through the huge ordeal of radiotherapy. After all, it might be the last time they would all be together.

They decided to spend the following weekend at Rainbow House, a country home in Great Bookham, Surrey, run by the Rainbow Trust, a charity for families with terminally ill and dying children.

Their first contact with the Rainbow Trust had been through Irene Hopper, who visited them at home and assessed their needs. Irene wasn't a great one for talking, but she obviously loved the three children.

It was a pleasant time away from the clinical smells of hospital. For Simon and Michelle it was a chance to play in the fields and enjoy a break with their parents and little brother.

They got to know a number of the carers at Rainbow House. There was Joyce Scallon, whom Ashley called 'Joyous'. With her cheerfulness she really did live up to Ashley's name for her. Jeanette Ward was another carer, slim, well spoken and very English. There were also Ken Crawford and Pat Keawn.

Arthur Kinge was another carer. Tall, bearded and built like a brick outhouse, Arthur was gentle yet could be sharp when he needed to be. A former ambulance driver, he and Andrew would spend hours playing swingball together. Unfortunately, because they were both so strong and competitive, the tennis ball would regularly part company with the string holding it to the post. Andrew felt bad about destroying the Rainbow Trust's property and bought them another one. Within a few minutes, he and Arthur had managed to destroy that one, too.

Sunday came, and the Fowle family went to the nearby farm. Simon, Michelle and Ashley loved the sheep, cows, goats and chickens. They especially enjoyed stroking the baby animals.

At the farm there was a wishing-well. Lots of the parents went there in desperation, throwing in a coin and making a wish that their son or daughter would live. Vivien wanted to use the chance to benefit Ashley, but she wasn't keen on the idea of good luck and making wishes.

Suddenly, she had an idea. Reaching into her purse she took out a silver coin and threw it into the well. Then, while the other parents made their wishes, she offered up a silent prayer. 'God, I want Ashley to get better somehow,' she prayed silently. 'Please show us the next step. Help us to know where we should go from here to get help for him.'

While Simon and Michelle played happily with the animals, Andrew and Vivien took Ashley in his pushchair into one of the farm buildings where there was a bookstall. One of the books on sale was *A Time to Heal,* by Beata Bishop (New English Library, 1985). In it, Beata Bishop talked about how a special diet known as Gerson Therapy had helped to control her malignant melanoma, the fastest-growing skin cancer. They bought a copy and packed it with their other things ready for the journey home.

Back at home in Northfleet, Kent, Vivien began browsing through the book. She wondered if God was showing her that 'the next step' in helping Ashley was to change his diet. She talked this over with Andrew and the next day he phoned the Gerson Institute in Bonita, California, where Gerson Therapy had originated.

They referred him to someone much closer to home, a Mrs L. Barty-Taylor of Edinburgh in Scotland. She had a ten-year-old son called Vivian (one of Ashley's middle names) who was on the diet. She was very helpful and even got her son to come to the phone. Young Vivian said the food he had to eat was yukky and disgusting but at least it was keeping his tumour under control.

In the course of the conversation, Mrs Barty-Taylor also mentioned a surgeon in the US called Dr Epstein who specialized in children's brain tumours. She had contacted him but, in the end, she didn't want her son having to go through surgery before trying the therapy.

'Maybe it's worth you contacting him,' she said to Andrew.

They were in a turmoil. People advocating the Gerson Therapy recommended that the patient had no treatment or surgery before beginning it. How could they say to the doctors: 'We don't want Ashley to have radiotherapy—we're going to try him on the Gerson method'?

In the end, after reading some more about the Gerson Therapy treatment, Andrew and Vivien felt they couldn't subject Ashley to the very restrictive diet involved. It included blended organic vegetable juices. The idea revolted them. Ashley was having enough trouble keeping *ordinary* food down, let alone this kind of thing.

In any case, it was now time to get ready for Ashley to be admitted to Guy's Hospital in London, ready to start his radiotherapy the following day.

Once more they made their way by train to London. As soon as Ashley was settled in, Andrew said goodbye and went home. He was tense and anxious but he was sure they were doing the right thing in agreeing to radiotherapy for Ashley. Vivien stayed with Ashley overnight ready for his radiotherapy in the morning.

There was to be one session a day during the week, with a break each weekend. Because of his young age and the fact that he had to be clamped to the table face down, Ashley had a mild general anaesthetic.

Once Ashley had succumbed to the effect of the anaesthetic, the radiographer would position him on the couch. Two beams of light were shone from the machine onto a point on Ashley's neck, which had been shaved. Then everyone would have to leave the room and the radiotherapy beam would be switched on.

For the next couple of minutes he was on his own, with Vivien and the radiographer watching through the protective glass barrier behind which they stood. Then the machine was switched off and the radiographer would go in and move it to a slightly different position, focus it with the light beams, and the process would begin again. This went on for a number of minutes until the radiotherapy was finished.

The staff played music during the treatment. It was mainly for the benefit of patients. In Ashley's case, unlike adults, he was unconscious, so he didn't benefit from it. Sometimes the music would be a bit slow and morbid. Vivien would get sick of it and ask for something a bit more cheerful.

Ashley, now three and a half years old, hated the radiotherapy sessions because of the fear of being put under general anaesthetic. It never seemed to get any easier.

He never related easily to the elderly anaesthetist, Dr Donald Gold. When it came time for Ashley's radiotherapy, Ashley would be lying on Vivien's lap and Dr Gold would suddenly say: 'Attack from behind, Ashley.'

Immediately the anaesthetist would thrust a rubber mask over Ashley's face. The plan was to anaesthetize him using a special mixture of gases that Dr Gold had invented. It knocked people out but had no long-lasting effect on them.

Such was Ashley's determination not to go to sleep that Ashley would hold his breath as soon as the mask was put on him. His breath-holding fits lasted only a few seconds but they were enough to show the doctor how determined he was to resist. Eventually, blue in the face, little Ashley would gasp for a breath and soon be knocked out by the anaesthetic.

After a time Dr Gold tried a different approach. Instead of the mask, he used a simple plastic tube that he would put near Ashley's face. Instinctively, Ashley knew it was there and would desperately try to resist the knock-out effect of the gas it was emitting.

Ashley decided to get his own back on Dr Gold. He had been given a new toy gun that shot lightweight foam darts. With the gun aiming at the door into the radiotherapy department, Ashley waited patiently for his victim. Various staff members went in and out of the door and still he held his fire.

Then Dr Gold appeared. Instantly, Ashley's finger squeezed the trigger and the dart shot out of the gun. It was a direct hit on his forehead. Dr Gold looked shocked as Ashley and several staff members burst out laughing. Ashley had triumphed.

'I hit him really good,' Ashley said later.

For the first two weeks of radiotherapy, Vivien slept on a fold-up bed next to Ashley's bed. It was an unsatisfactory arrangement. Vivien found it difficult to sleep. The ward was full of noises: children crying, heart monitors bleeping and nurses going about the routine care of young patients. Vivien would also wake up every time Ashley turned over in bed.

On Friday, 29 April, Ashley and his mother went home for the weekend. Andrew and Vivien decided that now would be a good chance to explain to Simon and Michelle what was happening with Ashley's treatment and how serious the situation had become.

Nine-year-old Simon took the news that Ashley was probably going to die worse than Michelle. He broke down and cried. For Michelle, aged six, it took much longer for the news to sink in. Perhaps they didn't fully understand what death meant: one of them rushed up to Ashley and said in a loud voice: 'Ashley, you're going to die!'

Back at the hospital, radiotherapy began again on Monday morning. It only lasted about half an hour. Once Ashley had recovered from the effects of the anaesthetic, he and Vivien had the rest of the day to do whatever they wanted. Ashley made friends with other children and spent a lot of his time in the playroom. Vivien filled her time with talking to other parents and to staff members.

Once a week Julie, the play specialist from Guy's, would organize a trip for the children. Trips had included visits to HMS Belfast, the Tower of London and Woburn Abbey. Sometimes the whole Fowle family would be able to go along.

Another week passed, and Vivien and Ashley were at home again. It was Friday, 6 May and Vivien had an appointment that afternoon with her family doctor. She was feeling depressed and suffering from dizzy spells.

Ashley's treatment was getting her down. She hated seeing him suffer like this.

In addition, being in the same room as Ashley wasn't helping her. For the two weeks since Ashley's treatment had started she hadn't been sleeping at all well at nights.

As she waited to be called into the consulting room, Vivien sat in the waiting room, praying silently about Ashley's situation. She didn't normally read in a waiting room. She had always found it soothing, almost comforting, just listening to others as they rustled the pages of their books and magazines.

This time, though, she reached her hand down and the very first thing she picked up was a small magazine. Looking at the cover she realized it was a copy of *Reader's Digest*, dated April 1993.

She noticed the usual kind of articles in the magazine—'Laughter, the Best Medicine', 'Hands Off Our BBC' and 'Ugliest Cat in the World'. But her eye was caught by that month's Book Choice. It was the 'triumphs of a trail-blazing neurosurgeon', and it was under the title 'I Don't Accept Children Dying'. The subject of the article was a grinning, white-haired American surgeon, Dr Fred Epstein, and his book was *Gifts of Time*.

That's who the woman from Edinburgh talked about! Vivien thought, her heart beating rapidly. *I wonder if this is God's way of telling me to contact him?*

She took the magazine to the receptionist.

'Could I take this magazine, please?' she asked. Then, in desperation, she corrected herself: 'No, I'm taking this magazine whether you want it or not!'

'That's fine,' the receptionist replied, trying her best not to be offended by this patient's bluntness. 'Take it. After all, it's only an old one.'

Vivien would have paid any amount of money to have it. She didn't have to. The receptionist was giving it to her free.

After her appointment with the doctor, she hurried home to read the article. Dr Epstein's speciality was operating on brain-stem tumours in children. That was exactly what Ashley had! Over many years, using the latest in laser and microsurgery equipment, Fred Epstein had mastered the delicate art of opening up the base of the skull and removing what he described as 'the enemy', the ugly mass of tumour tissue that had usually dogged the child's life for so long.

As a boy, Fred Epstein had had learning disabilities and wasn't successful academically. Yet he had been determined to be a doctor and, after many years of intensive training, had gone on to specialize in brain surgery. By 1985 he had become director of the newly-formed paediatric (child) neurosurgery division at New York University Medical Centre.

'Watching a tumour ravaging a child is like watching all the beauty of creation in reverse,' he said. 'Children weren't meant to die. I don't accept children dying—until I've tried everything. I take on cases that other neuro-surgeons shy away from because I don't believe in the "inevitable".'

Vivien drew in her breath as she read those words. *There really is hope for Ashley,* she thought.

In the article Dr Epstein said he always believed his highly skilled operations would save lives. 'Otherwise there is no point in the hope I offer to patients, no point in living with myself,' he wrote. 'What I do takes strong ego. I'm the best at what I do, and I never operate think-ing otherwise.'

On one occasion Fred Epstein was criticized by a fellow surgeon for visiting young patients in their homes and going to their celebrations. 'You get too involved. It's not good.'

'Not good for whom?' retorted Epstein. 'I know it's good for the parents. They tell me it is. They have to be able to feel hope.'

'How can you offer hope when there isn't any?'

'You have to believe,' Fred Epstein replied. 'Miracles do happen. I've seen them.'

A miracle—that's what Ashley needs! thought Vivien.

That weekend Vivien popped around to see her sister and showed herself in through the back door. Jackie was in her kitchen.

'Oh, hello, Viv,' said Jackie, pleased to see her. 'How's Ashley?'

'All right, I suppose.'

Jackie had been continuing to get up early in the mornings to pray for Ashley. Sometimes when she prayed she felt as if her prayer had already been answered. At other times, during her lowest moments, she would see how ill Ashley looked and would have doubts. She would pray: 'Why don't you put Viv out of her misery and hurry up and heal Ashley? But if it is your will that he dies, then please don't let him suffer.'

During one of Ashley's routine hospital visits Jackie had looked after Simon and Michelle. When Andrew came to pick them up, Jackie told him about her thoughts and prayers.

'I love and care a lot about Ashley,' she said, 'and I pray that God will heal him soon and stop his and Viv's suffering.'

Recently, though, something else had come to mind, and now seemed as good a time as any to tell Vivien about it.

'I don't know why, Viv, but I've had this thought that we're going to have to raise some money for you 'cos you're going to America.'

'Oh, really? It's funny you should say that 'cos I've just been reading this article about a doctor in New York who operates on children with brain-stem tumours.'

'Stop it. Hearing that makes me go all cold and tingly, 'cos that's just what I thought,' said Jackie.

'Ashley needs a miracle, Jackie. Somehow we've got to get him to New York.'

Vivien was sure this was the answer to Ashley's tumour. Now all that remained was to convince Andrew and the doctors.

8 McHappy House

On the following Monday Vivien and Ashley were back at Guy's Hospital ready for another week of radiotherapy. Later that same week, Andrew came to London and together they questioned the oncologist, Dr Joan Whitehead, about Dr Epstein.

'Apparently, he's operated on brain-stem tumours where other doctors haven't,' said Andrew. 'Could he be an option?'

'Well, he may be worth investigating. In the past, at parents' instigation, we've sent him scans and asked his opinion. He's always reached the same conclusion as our surgeons and hasn't suggested anything different. He got a lot of publicity from an article in *Reader's Digest*, wasn't it?'

'I've been reading it,' said Andrew.

'He's somewhat embarrassed about it because, as often happens, the journalists haven't got the story quite straight.'

'It says he cuts into the actual spinal tissue, venturing where no other surgeon has ventured,' said Andrew. 'This was about ten years ago.'

'I've seen it, thank you. I can't comment about the neurosurgery.'

'Why hasn't it happened over here?'

'From the letters we've had from him—and the comments from Dr Audrey, who knows him and has consulted with him in the past—we know he's a very careful neurosurgeon. It's difficult to project that in an article that's intended to catch the public eye.'

'So is it worth contacting him at all?'

'I wouldn't have thought so myself, but I wouldn't stop you. Perhaps the sensible thing is to talk to Dr Audrey and see what he says.'

They spoke to Dr Paul Audrey the same day.

'Cutting into his brain stem?' he said. 'It's not possible. Don't be silly!'

'Will you at least contact Dr Epstein in New York and discuss Ashley's case with him?'

'Of course. I'll gladly do that.'

It seemed he never did, even after constant phone calls to his secretary enquiring whether he had spoken to him. Andrew and Vivien were always given the same answer: 'Dr Audrey's been busy. I'll leave a message on his desk reminding him to call.'

It looked as if the idea of taking Ashley to the US for treatment had been a five-minute wonder. Perhaps Vivien had been clutching at straws. Now Andrew and Vivien had to get on with helping Ashley through the second half of his intensive course of radiotherapy.

Up to now Ashley had taken the treatment well, with none of the serious side effects his parents had been told about. The only thing he suffered from was a form of redness and peeling, like sunburn, on his ears and the back of his neck. Vivien put a soothing white cream on him as soon as he finished each session of radiotherapy.

Whenever Ashley went out at weekends Andrew and Vivien made sure he wore a hat to protect his skin from the sunlight. One time they forgot and took him outside without any protection. The result was that his ears blistered much worse than before.

After the first couple of weeks of camping in the ward next to Ashley's bed, Vivien had been thrilled to be offered a room with Ashley at the Ronald McDonald House, near Guy's, owned and managed by a charity called The Evelina Family Trust. This trust was established in 1986 to raise funds to build and run 'a home away from home' to enable families to be near children undergoing treatment at Guy's.

A place to stay for parents of sick children seemed a long way from the fast-food world of Big Macs and Chicken McNuggets. Yet McDonald's was an organization where much effort was put into helping sick children.

Ronald McDonald's Children's Charities was started in the US in 1984 as a memorial to Ray Kroc, founder of the McDonald's empire, who once said, 'We have an obligation to give something back to the communities that gave so much to us.' Five years later it was set up in the UK. Since then Ronald McDonald Houses had been built beside two of the leading hospitals, Guy's Hospital in London and Alder Hey Children's Hospital in Liverpool.

McDonald's staff inspired the public to contribute to corporate fund-raising initiatives and donated part of the proceeds to the Evelina Family Trust towards initial costs of establishing the house at Guy's. It was opened in June 1990 and accommodated sixteen families at any one time. Medical experts believe that children recover more quickly if their families are with them. Without the house, Andrew and Vivien would have had to pay huge accommodation costs or travel from their home near Gravesend, Kent, to central London every day. Or Vivien would have had to continue staying in the ward next to Ashley's bed, which was highly unsatisfactory. Staying at the house was free due to the Trust's continuing fund-raising efforts.

Even when he felt off colour after his radiotherapy, Ashley didn't lose his sense of humour. Once in Ronald McDonald House he and Vivien were in an elevator when a very obese man—another resident—stepped in. Vivien smiled politely. Ashley, on the other hand, looked up into the man's face.

'Excuse me,' he asked.

'Yes.'

'Are you Mr Blobby?' he asked innocently, thinking of the round pink-and-yellow character that appeared with Noel Edmunds on BBC television's 'Noel's House Party'.

Vivien was totally embarrassed. The worst thing was that she had to have breakfast with this man every morning for the next three weeks. They tended to avoid each other after that.

About halfway through Ashley's radiotherapy, Dave Webster, leader of the church Andrew and Vivien had begun to attend, invited Andrew to a meeting for church leaders in Sidcup, Kent. During the meeting, people prayed for Andrew. Back at home, he was unloading some things from the washing machine when suddenly he was overcome with fits of laughter for no apparent reason. All the feelings of guilt about his failures and heaviness about the situation with Ashley left him. They were replaced with a peace he had never known before. He felt God was saying to him: 'I'll take your burdens. You don't need to carry them any more.'

Ashley's treatment finished at last on Thursday, 2 June. Andrew travelled to London to collect Vivien and Ashley together with all their things. At last the whole family could be back together again. But it was a very different boy from the one who had started treatment six weeks earlier.

During the last couple of weeks, Ashley had got much worse as a result of the radiotherapy. He had been walking up to two weeks before the end of radiotherapy. Then he became too weak. He was unable even to crawl around the house. His whole right side had deteriorated and he had lost the use of his right arm, which had previously been his stronger side. Before treatment he had been able to draw with his right hand. Now he couldn't even pick up a pencil with it, and he had to begin learning how to be left-handed.

He had long since stopped eating. Everything he tried to eat he brought up again. The doctors described him as 'anorexic'. Andrew and Vivien had to feed him through a nasal gastric tube, which meant hooking him up to a feed pump for twelve hours a night. The liquid he was given was highly concentrated, with 400 calories in one small bottle. Andrew tried some once and thought it was quite pleasant.

The purpose of such concentrated liquid was to build Ashley's weight up as quickly as possible, but even that wasn't working. Andrew and Vivien had to reduce his feed to eight hours a night because he was being so sick.

Ashley wasn't a big child to start off with, but during radiotherapy his weight plummeted from 28lb (12.7kg) to a mere 12lb (5.5kg). He had hardly any hair and had become very thin and gaunt-looking, just like a child suffering the advanced stages of AIDS.

All Andrew and Vivien could see was their little boy worse after treatment than before. He continued to deteriorate. His breathing became more heavy and he grew tired quickly. His parents were becoming more and more concerned.

Three weeks after Ashley's treatment finished, he had a routine appointment with the paediatrician at the Livingstone Hospital in Dartford, Kent. Ashley was checked over and declared as well as could be expected after such major treatment.

The following Sunday, 26 June, was a day Andrew and Vivien would never forget. The two of them, along with their nine-year-old son Simon, were baptized in a large tank of water at Emmanuel Baptist Church in Gravesend. Their church had borrowed the building especially for the occasion. Baptism was a vital part of their new commitment to God. The water was icy cold but it was otherwise a good time, subdued only by Ashley's desperate condition.

Their first appointment at Guy's Hospital came on Tuesday 5 July. Nearly five weeks had gone by since radiotherapy, and still Ashley showed little sign of improvement. They were due to see the tall neurologist Professor James Richardson again. 'Imagine having to see *him* on my birthday!' said Vivien.

After examining him, Professor Richardson said that, considering all Ashley had gone through, he wasn't doing too badly.

Vivien was far from convinced. If Ashley wasn't doing too badly, why had his disabilities increased? Finally, towards the end of the appointment, she plucked up courage to ask the question that was burning in her.

'Professor Richardson, if Ashley's tumour were to go, would he get some of his strength back in his arms and legs?'

'Mrs Fowle, Ashley's tumour will *never* go away,' he said without emotion. 'It'll be there throughout his whole life.'

The reply cut Vivien to the core of her being. There seemed no hope for Ashley. Even the doctors had now written him off.

Back at home, the stress and mental torment caused by Ashley's illness were beginning to have an effect on Andrew and Vivien's relationship. Arguments became more frequent, and everyday life was like trudging up a very steep hill when they were already exhausted physically and mentally.

Despite the way they felt, Andrew and Vivien started attending a series of weekly classes called Joining the Church. A week later, on Saturday 23 July, it was Ashley's fourth birthday. Andrew and Vivien wanted to give him a memorable time. They tried not to think too far into the future, but Andrew began to wonder if this birthday would be Ashley's last.

They invited a few friends around and had a sort of party. Ashley was in a bad way with his nasal gastric tube. He was still being sick and he wouldn't even try to walk or crawl. He was so weak that Vivien had to hold him up during musical chairs. At food time, he just looked on as everyone tucked into his party food. After much persuasion he tried a little bit of birthday cake, but refused to eat anything else.

At four o'clock one morning Vivien's sister, Jackie, woke up feeling worried. She began to relive the time four and a half years before when she spoke to her husband after Vivien's ultrasonic scan showed that Ashley was still in her womb.

'I've had this thought,' Jackie told him at the time. 'The baby's going to be a boy. He'll get ill, but he's going to get better; he won't die.'

Her husband hadn't taken it seriously. 'Don't say things like that,' he said. 'It's not nice.'

'Well, I'm telling you now so when it happens you'll believe me.'

Now she was really worried in case what she had said was coming true. Maybe, after all, it wasn't a nice thing to say. Perhaps she had somehow even *caused* her nephew's problems.

At her lowest point, early that summer morning, Jackie opened her Bible and came across similar words spoken by Jesus to his disciples: 'I am telling you now before it happens, so that when it does happen you will believe.'

On Saturday, 30 July Andrew and Vivien, together with the three children, joined thousands of other people at Stoneleigh Bible Week, near Coventry in the Midlands. They borrowed a reliable car from Graham and Carol Lucas, friends of theirs who went to their church. Graham was a 'banana man'—he bought and sold bananas—and Carol was a teacher.

Through a rental company in Essex they had arranged a caravan for the Fowle family to stay in for the week. The caravan had to be sited near the buildings so they had a power point. This was because Ashley was still being fed by nasal gastric tube and they needed electricity to power his pump.

What would have been an enjoyable break for the whole family turned into a nightmare when one evening Ashley started vomiting up blood. That night the gastric nasal tube came out and the end of it was bright red.

Andrew and Vivien were overcome by terror. Had the tube punctured the lining of his stomach? Would he bleed internally? Was this the beginning of the end for their little boy?

Ashley had survived so much. Was he now destined to die in this field, among thousands of other campers, in the middle of nowhere?

9 Somewhere Under the Rainbow

Andrew phoned Guy's Hospital and explained to them about the blood-soaked nasal gastric tube and the fact that Ashley was vomiting up blood.

'How many days do you have left of your holiday?' the doctor asked.

'Just two.'

'OK. It sounds like his stomach may have become ulcerated or perforated by the tube.'

'Is that serious?'

'No, I don't think so. Leave the tube out and take him to the first-aid post at the campsite for the doctor to check him. See if you can get Ashley to eat. Then finish your holiday and come to Guy's on Monday.'

It was a relief for Andrew and Vivien, as well as for Ashley, not to have the bother of the gastric tube. That night they all managed to get some good, sound sleep.

The next day was the last one of the Bible Week. Vivien decided to go to the final meeting, while Andrew was babysitting at the caravan. There were thousands of others at the meeting. During it, their babysitter Lee Rawlinson introduced Vivien to a man who told her how his wife had been miraculously healed of cancer when he prayed and placed his hands on her.

Vivien asked him to pray for her. The man prayed over Vivien's hands so that when she put them on Ashley and prayed, he would get better, too.

On Saturday, as they packed to leave, she prayed for Ashley. From that moment on he didn't vomit up any more blood.

The following Monday they went to Guy's Hospital in London. Although Ashley was no longer vomiting up blood, he was still being sick after almost everything he ate. He was losing weight and Vivien thought he looked almost like a skeleton, with his eyes sunken into darkened sockets.

The doctors decided to keep him in overnight. They tried him on a different anti-sickness drug, which seemed to help.

Ashley also had another MRI scan. This showed a lot of swelling around the site of the tumour, so much so that the tumour wasn't even visible on the film. The doctors said that the swelling was probably caused by the radiotherapy and should reduce in time. They believed this was why Ashley's weight had been deteriorating. They likened the effect of radiotherapy on the tumour to hitting your thumb with a hammer—it becomes painful and swells up. Andrew and Vivien were told that tumours sometimes reacted like that when they were treated with radiotherapy.

The doctors decided to start Ashley on a course of steroid treatment to reduce the swelling, which would in turn relieve his symptoms. Then they would do another scan after six weeks. The swelling should have subsided by then, they explained reassuringly.

Almost the minute Ashley started taking the steroids his appetite improved 100 per cent and he began to put on weight. Vivien breathed a huge sigh of relief.

With Ashley's immediate problems under control, Andrew and Vivien took a much-needed week's break at Flint House, a police convalescent home in Goring, Oxfordshire. Simon and Michelle were looked after by relatives while Ashley was under the care of Tina Norris, a domiciliary carer from Rainbow Trust. At last, Andrew and Vivien could relax and try to find some relief from the stress they were under.

During the week they were in a minibus on a day trip to Windsor Castle when Andrew suddenly got a vivid picture in his mind of the minibus driving up a steep hill, at the top of which the road bent sharply to the left and levelled off. In the picture Andrew could see the minibus going around the corner towards a long line of cars coming from the opposite direction. Overtaking this line of cars was a white van. The minibus driver was being forced to swerve to avoid a collision and sliding down a steep bank on its side, eventually being stopped by trees. Andrew pictured himself impaled on a tree branch inside the bus, with blood everywhere.

'God, save us,' he prayed quietly. 'Prevent this from happening to us.'

Soon the scene became familiar. Although Andrew had never been to that part of England, he recognized the hill and sat in anticipation of what would happen when they reached the top. Sure enough, as they rounded the bend, they were confronted by a line of cars being overtaken by a white van. The minibus driver braked and the van only just managed to squeeze back into the line of cars, avoiding a major collision.

Andrew recalled later: 'I honestly believe that if God hadn't given me that vision and I hadn't prayed for safety, the picture that was so vivid in my mind would have become a reality.'

Their break finished, they returned home to the routine of caring for their seriously ill child. Vivien couldn't get out of her mind the *Reader's Digest* article she had read about Dr Fred Epstein. While Ashley was having his radiotherapy she had come across another article about Epstein's pioneering work in New York. She had been at a low point and her friend from Northfleet, Gay Males, whose son Jason also had a tumour, took Ashley out for a time. As Vivien sat alone in the hospital, praying, she picked up a newspaper and flicked through it. There, on the fifth page, was a story about Sally Djemil, who had been flown from London to New York for Dr Epstein to remove her brain tumour.

Vivien seemed to hear a voice in her mind. 'I've told you once through the woman in Edinburgh. I told you twice through *Reader's Digest*. Now I've told you a third time. I'm not telling you again.' It seemed to Vivien that God was pointing them strongly towards treatment for Ashley under Dr Epstein in New York.

Another article came to light about a little girl, Alicia McCluckie, from Poynton, Cheshire, who had also had revolutionary treatment in New York. Andrew and Vivien showed the two articles to the doctors at Guy's and a nurse even photocopied them for the records. The hospital staff maintained that such articles were always over-exaggerated by the Press. People never saw what these patients were like after they returned to the UK, when the National Health Service had to repair the mess left by the American doctors.

While Vivien believed that God was showing them the next step in Ashley's treatment, Andrew was inclined to believe their own doctors. After all, they were in London, reputedly one of the best medical centres in the world. If the doctors in London couldn't operate on Ashley, no one could, he reasoned.

Finally, after Vivien continued to enthuse about this possible American treatment, Andrew decided to contact Dr Epstein in New York. He couldn't believe it when he got right through to the doctor in person. Andrew explained to him as best he could about Ashley's difficulties. Dr Epstein said he would need to see Ashley's MRI scans before he could make any comment.

Getting the scans was a huge task. Andrew and Vivien asked repeatedly for copies of them, and each time they met another difficulty. Weeks went by and they hadn't even got an application form to get the records sent.

One day Vivien's sister, Jackie, had a thought that broke her normal routine. On Mondays Jackie would switch on the telephone answering machine and not see anyone. It was her day for getting things done around the house. Now a single parent with four young boys to care for, she felt she needed that time. She wrote a list of things to do on that particular day and nothing got in the way of that list.

On this particular Monday a thought came into her mind that she needed to put off her list until Tuesday. She dropped her children at school and got home to find a message waiting for her on the answering machine.

'Help, Jackie. I need to see you.' It was Vivien.

Jackie had been working on autopilot since the news that Ashley might not survive much longer. She rushed around to see her sister, who showed her a leaflet she had been sent by the hospital. It was about hospices and had a picture of children dying of various incurable illnesses. The hospital had suggested that, when the time came, Ashley could be taken to one of these places.

'I sat there looking at this leaflet crying my eyes out,' recalled Jackie later. 'I was supposed to be the strong one for my sister and I was in floods of tears.'

Jackie started to get really angry because the consultants had wasted time by not getting the scans sent off to Dr Epstein. It wasn't her normal kind of anger when she blew up at the children for being naughty. This was indignation.

'I can't tolerate this situation any more,' she said to Vivien. 'Give me the names of the consultants and I'll phone them up and sort them out.'

'You can't do that, Jackie. They won't treat Ashley any more if you upset them.'

'Not treat him? It's your right under the National Health Service to have him treated. Now, give me the names and phone numbers.'

Angrily she phoned up the office of first one, then the other consultant.

'We want the scans of Ashley sent to America.'

'Well, they'll have to be photocopied and that'll take two or three weeks.'

Photocopied? Since when could films be photocopied?

'That's not good enough.'

'We *do* have other things to do, you know.'

'Look, Ashley's seriously ill. I want to speak to Mr Polecat and I want to speak to him now!' she demanded angrily.

'Mr Polecat? Oh, you mean Mr Pollard.'

'Whatever, get him for me.'

'Look, I don't like your attitude.'

'That's OK. I don't like yours either. Now I want to speak to the engineer, not the oily rag.'

By this time Vivien's tears had turned into laughter as her sister, in her inimitable way, was charging through the red tape like a bull in a china shop. By the end of the various phone conversations they were both laughing hysterically.

After a few more phone calls asking about the complaints procedure, Jackie was told to phone the manager of the hospital where Ashley's records were stored.

When she got through, she told the manager: 'I'm not here to complain. All I want is Ashley's scans.'

'I can't do anything unless there's been a complaint,' the manager said. They were in a no-win situation. She didn't want to complain, yet that seemed to be the only way to get any action.

Something must have happened, though, because within a few days an application form to request the records arrived. Once that was completed, Andrew and Vivien had to sit back and wait.

On Monday, 10 October, following another MRI scan, the doctors said that Ashley's tumour had swollen even further. His face had also now ballooned up as a result of the steroids.

'We believe that the tumour has changed its spots and is more vigorous in its growth,' Dr Joan Whitehead announced gloomily. 'We now think the swelling we're seeing is the tumour itself, not the result of the radiotherapy.'

In order to determine what they were now dealing with, the doctors wanted to do a second biopsy, certainly within the next couple of weeks. They thought the continued deterioration in Ashley's condition was because the tumour had started to grow more rapidly.

'If that's the case, Ashley will be severely disabled in the next six to twelve months,' said Dr Graham Pollard, the neurosurgeon.

'What do you mean by "severely disabled"?'

'No one can say for certain. But bear in mind that the tumour is situated next to the nerves that control the body's vital functions like swallowing, the heart and the lungs.'

Andrew and Vivien had been warned when Ashley was first diagnosed with a tumour of the brain stem that he would eventually suffer heart, breathing and swallowing problems. Now the time seemed to be rapidly approaching. Already, his breathing was heavy and laboured. They weren't at all sure what might happen next. Maybe with this operation it might be possible to remove the tumour. It was a slim hope, but Andrew had to try.

'If you did a biopsy, would you remove as much of the tumour as possible?' he asked.

'When I last went into Ashley's brain stem in March,' Dr Pollard said, 'I was only able to remove enough for the biopsy because it was just too dangerous to remove any more. I don't believe it will be any different this time. In fact, I believe it would be too detrimental to Ashley even to try.'

Vivien was livid. 'I don't want you to do a biopsy. I want Dr Epstein to look at him.'

'I really don't think this doctor can do it,' Dr Pollard said.

'Think?' asked Vivien. 'You did say think? Think isn't good enough. I want to *know*. If a bloke falls on the floor and you're not a doctor, would you just stand there because you don't think you can help him? Of course not! You'd get down and try to resuscitate him.'

'Yes, I guess I'd try.'

'That's exactly what I'm asking you to do. Just try.'

Andrew felt he had to apologize for Vivien's attitude. 'Vivien's got it into her head that this doctor in America can operate on Ashley. Can you for our peace of mind send the scans? If he says no, he can't do it, then at least we've tried. Then we can forget about it and get on with the biopsy here.'

'You realize it will cost £50 to send them?'

The doctors told Andrew and Vivien they were being foolish in delaying the biopsy as they didn't know what the tumour was doing. It was urgent to go ahead as quickly as possible because Ashley was deteriorating fast. Dr Epstein was no better a doctor than they were, and the scans would be on his desk for two or three weeks before he even looked at them.

'We want Ashley's scans sent to Dr Epstein in New York straight away,' Andrew insisted.

'It's not a matter of just putting them in an envelope and sending them,' one doctor said. 'They have to be copied and presented in a way that Dr Epstein can understand. That, of course, takes time.'

After the meeting Andrew phoned Dr Fred Epstein in New York. 'If I bring the scans over personally, will you look at them?'

'Yes, I'll look at them straight away,' he replied.

Andrew then telephoned Guy's Hospital to say he wanted to take them personally to New York.

They weren't happy. 'You'd just be acting as a courier,' one doctor said. 'It'd cost you a lot more to do that, and Dr Epstein wouldn't be able to make a decision while you waited. He'd need to consult with other doctors, which would take time. We can get them sent across in forty-eight hours, probably quicker.'

Eventually, after a lot of insisting on Andrew's part, the doctors reluctantly agreed to send them in the next forty-eight hours.

Two days later, Andrew and Vivien received Ashley's medical records, minus the all-important scans. Several weeks had gone by since they had first applied for them.

Finally, on Wednesday, 19 October 1994, a doctor from Guy's Hospital in London phoned Vivien to say that the scans were about to be sent off. Nine days had now gone by since their meeting with the doctors.

'Do you happen to have the address in New York where they should be sent?' she asked.

'No,' said Vivien. She was surprised at the request, because the doctors had told her and Andrew that they sent scans regularly to the US. 'But I can contact Dr Epstein's office and get it for you.'

'Thanks,' she replied.

Vivien started to phone New York University Medical Centre. Tina Norris and Jackie were standing beside Vivien to give her some support.

'Vivien, you know the address. You've got the address written down somewhere,' said Jackie. 'It's New York and it's got the numbers 1, 1 and 6 in it.'

'I haven't got that written down.'

'Oh, never mind, Vivien. Shut up, Jackie,' she said out loud to herself.

No one was more surprised than Vivien when, a short time later, they found that the zip code of the New York University Medical Centre was 10016. The numbers 1, 1 and 6 were there exactly as Jackie had said.

Jackie spent as much time at Vivien's house as she could. She knew her sister hated using the phone yet was having to spend much of her time on it. Each day, Jackie would ring the medical centre in New York to check if Ashley's scans had arrived. She became very friendly with the man in the mail room, who always tried to be helpful.

'Oh, hi, ma'am. It's you again. No, they're not here yet,' he would say cheerfully.

Eventually it emerged that the scans had been wrongly labelled and were stuck in customs. It took four days and several transatlantic phone calls for them to be released. Then Jackie asked for them to be sent by courier to the hospital.

That mailman she had negotiated with during this time was their lifeline to the hospital and played a big part in getting help for Ashley. 'I'd love to meet him one day,' Jackie said later.

Rainbows, with their promise of hope, had become very important to Vivien during this nailbiting wait. One Sunday during the time when Ashley had been having his radiotherapy, she had prayed: 'God, show me a rainbow to let me know that Ashley will be all right.' Later that same day she was in a bus going to Guy's with Ashley

RIGHT: Simon (6) and Michelle (3) on holiday in the Canaries in 1991.

ABOVE: Andrew and Vivien's first child, Elizabeth Anne Louise, died a cot death in 1984.

RIGHT: Ashley aged one.

BELOW: Ashley at Rainbow House, Great Bookham, in May 1994. His hair loss is due to radiotherapy.

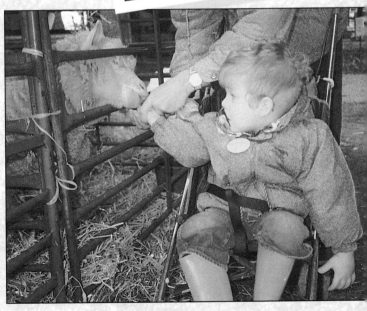

BELOW: Ashley's older sister and brother Michelle and Simon in late summer 1993.

LEFT: Ashley in Fort Gardens, Gravesend, in the summer of 1993, sitting on the bomb recovered from the garden of Vivien's parents.

LEFT: Ashley's protective helmet after it had shrunk and been given to Andrew's Mum's teddy bear.

BELOW: Ashley in New York in November 1994.

ABOVE: Vivien, Ashley and Andrew with Michelle and Simon on 30 October 1994, the day they left for New York.

ABOVE: First night in the NY University Medical Centre.

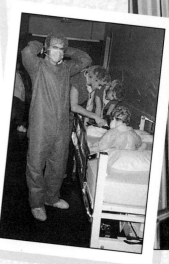

RIGHT: Andrew and Ashley preparing for the operation.

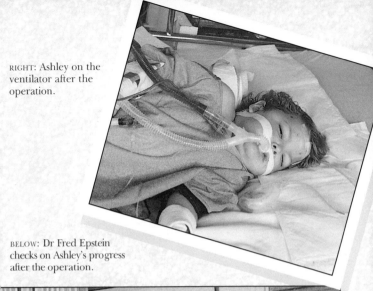

RIGHT: Ashley on the ventilator after the operation.

BELOW: Dr Fred Epstein checks on Ashley's progress after the operation.

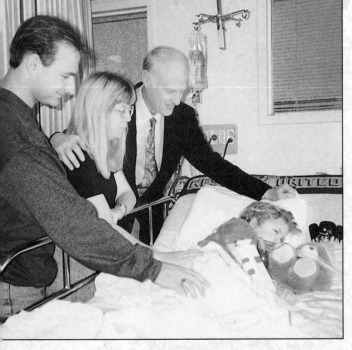

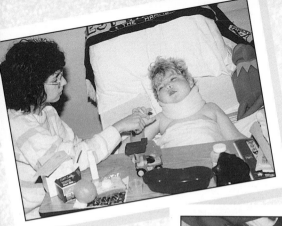

LEFT: Ashley receiving occupational therapy, his West Ham scarf proudly displayed. The neck brace was to be the cause of further complications.

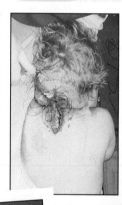

RIGHT: Ashley's wound after it had been cleaned out, showing the bootlace stitches.

BELOW: After the operation, Ashley received physiotherapy from Christy Worsoe.

ABOVE: With the Tigger who came to breakfast.

LEFT: Ashley at Walt Disney World in Florida. Ashley met Mickey and Minnie Mouse.

BELOW: Ashley with his parents after the ceremony in which he switched on the Christmas lights at Walt Disney World.

ABOVE: Simon and Michelle give Ashley a hug before he sets off for his first day at school in January 1995 (Daily Mail).

BELOW: The event that nearly didn't happen——Ashley's first day at school (Daily Mail).

ABOVE: Ashley and Vivien, six months after the operation, at Northfleet Carnival.

after the weekend at home. Suddenly, she saw another bus covered in painted rainbows.

'No, I don't mean that kind,' Vivien said under her breath. 'I want to see a *real* rainbow.'

At Guy's Hospital the walls had been covered in rainbows that the children had painted.

'No, they must have been there last week! That's not what I'm looking for. I asked for a real rainbow, God, not this artificial stuff.'

In London she had gone for a walk and seen a cafe called The Rainbow Tree.

'Look, I've had enough of this,' she prayed in exasperation. 'I want a rainbow *in the sky*.'

Jackie, too, had been looking for a rainbow to cheer up her sister. On Tuesday 25 October, after the scans had been sent to New York, she was gazing out of her house. 'Please, God. Let Ashley be all right,' she prayed.

Outside it had been sunny but now it started to rain slightly. She ran up to her sons' bedroom and looked out of their window. There, over the top of Vivien's house, she distinctly saw a rainbow.

'Look, boys,' she said to her children. 'That rainbow's for Ashley.'

The rainbow lasted just a few seconds and then began to fade.

She phoned Vivien right away. 'Quick, Viv, there's a rainbow over your house. I'm sure Ashley's going to be all right. Oh, I'm being silly. Don't take any notice of me. Still, you never know, do you?'

Five minutes later there was a phone call.

'Mrs Fowle?'

'Yes.'

'This is the New York University Medical Centre. I'm phoning to say that Ashley's scans have arrived and are on Dr Epstein's desk.'

'Oh, good! I'm so glad they've arrived.'

'Dr Epstein will probably take them home this evening and look at them overnight.'

Vivien rang Jackie straight away with the good news.

'Jackie, guess what?'

'What? What? Come on!'

'The scans are on his desk right this minute.'

'Stop it! I knew that rainbow was there for some reason.'

After that it was another nailbiting wait, this time for Dr Epstein to phone back with his decision. Vivien and Jackie were ringing each other every few minutes asking: 'Do you think he can do it?'

Andrew and Vivien didn't sleep well that night. The following day, Wednesday 26 October, Andrew went to work while Vivien tried her best to make the time pass quickly.

Tina from the Rainbow Trust came to spend time with Vivien. She was a great help and source of comfort. Each time the phone rang, Vivien got into such a state she could hardly speak, let alone answer the phone. Tina helped her each step of the way. Usually it was just Jackie at the other end of the line, asking for the umpteenth time if there was any news.

By the afternoon, Vivien was a nervous wreck. To keep herself occupied she decided to defrost the fridge. Tina was helping her and they were both getting soaked. Suddenly the phone rang and Tina stood beside Vivien as she picked up the receiver.

'Hello. This is the New York University Medical Centre. Is that Mrs Fowle?'

'Y-e-s.'

'I have Dr Epstein for you. Will you take the call?'

Vivien's heart skipped a beat and she gulped deeply. 'Er—yes.' This was it! The moment of truth had arrived. What would he say?

There was a long pause and several clicks as the operator made the connection. As she waited she thought: *I can't handle this if it's bad news. Where are we going to go from here if he can't do it? Do I want to take this call or not?* Her heart beat wildly as the time dragged on.

Suddenly, there was a deep, resonant American voice on the other end of the line. It sounded similar to the legendary film star Charlton Heston.

'Hello, ma'am.'

'Hello.'

'This is Dr Epstein speaking.'

'Yes. I'm Vivien Fowle, Ashley's mother.'

'Now, your child Ashley—is that a boy or a girl?'

'A boy.'

'OK, good. I have his scans in front of me. This is a typical brain-stem tumour of the type we see regularly over here. I deal with quite a few of these.'

'Oh, yes.'

'This isn't an uncommon tumour. I deal with cases from all over the world. I can tell by looking at the scans, and from the tumour's location, that the bulk of it isn't cancerous.'

He doesn't know what he's talking about! thought Vivien. *I know it's cancer, and that's it.*

'It's certainly not inoperable over here,' Dr Epstein continued.

'You mean you can operate on him?'

'Yes, ma'am, I can do it.'

'Really?' She felt absolutely thrilled.

'When can you come over with Ashley?'

'When do you want him?'

'Well, ma'am, today's Wednesday. My next available operating day is next Tuesday. I can clear my schedule for that day if you can get him here. Will that suit you?'

Tuesday. That was only six days away! How could she and Andrew get Ashley over to New York by then? They had trouble enough paying the household bills, let alone buying plane tickets. They didn't even have Ashley's name on their passports. Vivien's mind was racing.

'Ma'am, are you still there? Ma'am?'

'Er—yes, I'm here.'

'Can you make it on Tuesday?'

'Yes, we can,' said Vivien instinctively. Somehow they must.

'Good. I'll hand you over to my secretary to make the arrangements.'

Vivien was overwhelmed by what she had just heard. She was so dizzy with excitement that she couldn't continue the conversation with the secretary. Instead, she passed the receiver to Tina, who took down the details.

A few minutes later, Vivien rang Andrew to tell him the exciting news. It was the first good news he had heard in ages and suddenly he felt alive again. He was working in the local Neighbourhood Watch office with another officer, Mick Wright. By now it was 3.15 in the afternoon.

He said to Mick: 'Guess what? Epstein's phoned to say he can do it! But it's going to cost $47,500. How I'm going to raise that amount I just don't know.'

'Go and have a chat with the chief. Tell him about it and he might have some ideas.'

Andrew went straight upstairs and knocked on the door of Chief Superintendent Richard John Rixon.

'Excuse me, sir.'

'Yes?'

'I've just come to let you know that Dr Epstein has phoned my wife and told her that he can do the operation on Ashley.'

'Good. How much is all this going to cost?'

'At least $47,500, sir. That's £35,000. We'll have to do some fundraising to get it.'

'Well, what are you doing here at work? You'd better get home and start raising money. And I don't want to see you back in this station until your son's better!' he said bluntly.

While all this had been happening, Jackie's dad had called around to see Jackie and the boys. Her boys had a lot of energy and he suggested that a walk in the countryside would help them let off steam. It was ideal, though Jackie hadn't wanted to miss that victorious moment when Dr Epstein phoned to say he could do it.

They were walking in a field and her children were covered in mud. It was unusual for her to let them get so messy. The reason she was ignoring them was because she was thinking about her niece Elizabeth who had died in her cot so young. As she thought about Elizabeth, she prayed silently, urgently: 'Please, God, let Ashley be all right.'

Suddenly, she turned to her dad. 'What's the time, Dad?' she asked.

'What do you want to know that for? Are you bored already?'

'No, Dad. I need to know the time.'

'Well—let's see—it's ten to three.'

'I just thought I'd let you know that Dr Epstein's phoned to say he's going to do the operation.'

'Oh, yeah. Who told you that, then?'

'God, I guess.'

'Yeah. All right,' he said, with a mocking laugh.

'Remember that. Ten to three.'

'Yeah, sure.'

They got back to her house to find a note on the back door. By now it was about 4.30 on a dark, damp October day. *Jackie, come round urgently. Vivien.*

Jackie asked her dad to take care of the children for a while and raced across the road.

'Epstein's going to do it, isn't he!' she announced as she threw open the back door.

'Yes, but how did you know?'

'God told me while I was in the middle of a field! What time did Epstein phone?'

'Ten to three.'

10 Escape to New York

The phone call from New York set the whole family in a whirl. How could they raise £35,000 and get Ashley to a New York operating theatre within six days?

Andrew recalls:
I left the Neighbourhood Watch office as soon as I had been in to see Chief Superintendent Rixon.

Once home, I got straight on the phone to Sue Roberton at Police Welfare to tell her the exciting news. The welfare people had helped us earlier in Ashley's life when he was diagnosed as having hydrocephalus. They had also been there later when his mobility deteriorated as a result of the radiotherapy.

When we had first thought of going to New York for Ashley's treatment I had contacted Sue and asked about possible financial help. She had approached the Kent Police Benevolent Fund, who initially said: 'Wait and see what Epstein says.' Now she approached them a second time.

The following morning, Thursday, they had an emergency meeting to discuss Ashley's case. They said they would contribute to the expense if necessary, but they would first try to raise the money by public appeal. If they didn't raise enough, they would lend us the money. Because of the vast amount involved, though, they would want it paid back afterwards by a regular deduction from my wages over several years. It would leave me with financial difficulties, but what else could I do?

The benevolent fund decided to launch the 'Ashley to America' appeal that afternoon, starting the appeal rolling with their own generous donation of £5,000. The appeal would be officially launched at 4.45pm that day, Thursday, 27 October 1994.

A Press notice was faxed to national newspapers, radio and TV. It had the headline: Help Save Ashley's Life.

'This is Ashley's last chance,' I was quoted in the Press notice as saying. 'He's a lively, loving and articulate boy. We will do anything to get him the treatment he desperately needs.'

I got a phone call from Sue Roberton saying they had agreed to go public with the appeal fund. 'Expect a TV crew on your doorstep at five o'clock,' she told me.

Meanwhile, I phoned Dr Joan Whitehead out of courtesy to let her know we were going to go public, but she wasn't available at the time. She returned my call later that day.

'What's going on?' she asked.

I told her that Dr Epstein had phoned yesterday and said he could do the operation. We needed to raise a large amount of money to finance the operation in New York because she, Dr Pollard and Professor Richardson had told us Ashley's tumour couldn't be operated on. 'We felt we had no other choice than to go to the US,' I explained.

'I think you're rushing things. Anyway, how could Dr Epstein make a decision to operate based on the little information he's been given?'

'He seems happy with it.'

'Well, I think it would have been ethical for him at least to contact me to discuss Ashley's case. After all, we know Ashley better than anyone else.'

Fred Epstein had tried to contact her the day before but she wasn't available. I suggested she give me a phone number where she could be contacted so I could give it to him. Later, after speaking with Dr Epstein, she phoned me back.

'I've just had a very long and interesting conversation with Dr Epstein,' she said. 'I'm happy with what he's told me. He's obviously very experienced in his field.'

She had made a concession. Now I wanted to know her opinion about going to New York. 'What,' I asked, 'would you do if you were in my position, with no other hope for Ashley?'

'I can't speak as a mother, because I don't have any children,' she said. 'But speaking as a surrogate mother to many of my patients, I would probably go for it.'

Because of delays, the TV crew didn't actually turn up until six. After that, it was just chaos. From that moment on, our lives were turned upside down as we were thrust into the public eye. Our feet didn't touch the ground.

The story of Ashley and his need for life-saving surgery caught the public's imagination. We had TV crews from all over—Meridian, BBC, Sky Television, cable networks—lining up in our hall and outside the front door to interview us, one after the other.

That evening the phone didn't stop ringing. Sue came round and took over answering the phone so that Vivien and I could do the interviews. Even then, the TV people had to keep shooting extra takes because the phone was in our sitting room, where we did the interviews.

While we were busy taking phone calls and doing interviews for TV and radio, the hotline was being co-ordinated by Inspector Jan Berry, chairperson of the Kent Police Benevolent Fund. She told reporters: 'Our prayers and thoughts are with Ashley.' Hundreds of off-duty Kent police officers and people on training courses took it in turns to man the credit card hotline. Members of the public sent in donations from everywhere.

BBC television rang us up and invited us to appear the next day on 'Good Morning... with Anne and Nick', the daytime show compèred by Anne Diamond and Nick Owen.

'We can't,' I told them. 'We've got to go to the Passport Office tomorrow to get Ashley's name put on our passports.'

Because it would be Friday tomorrow and we planned to travel on Sunday, we had to get it done that day.

'Don't worry. We'll take care of it,' said the man at the BBC. 'We'll order a car to take you there if you'll allow us to come to the Passport Office and film you collecting the passport.'

'Sounds good,' I said.

'We'll take you to the BBC studio and you'll appear by satellite link on "Good Morning... with Anne and Nick". Then we'll take you to the Passport Office.'

In the event, because of the influence of having the BBC film crew with us, we were in and out of the Passport Office within an hour. Yet the electronic board in the waiting area was informing people that there was a waiting time of three and a half hours.

We saw the BBC report of the visit to the Passport Office on TV later that day. It was made to look like live action. The only trouble was, we had to walk through the door into the Passport Office three times to get it just right!

Saturday, as it turned out, was just as busy as Friday—only it started much earlier. One reporter from a radio station slept in his Volvo Estate overnight until seven in the morning, waiting to be the first to interview us. I spent the whole morning and much of the afternoon sitting on the arm of the chair being interviewed on the phone. I had my breakfast and dinner sitting there talking between mouthfuls.

The previous evening Vivien's dad had gone out and bought us some Kentucky Fried Chicken. It went cold so someone heated it up for us. On Saturday, Vivien heated it up and it went cold again! Eventually, we managed to eat it—reheated again. I know reheated chicken can cause food poisoning, but we were taking emergency action. It certainly didn't affect us.

Once, when the phone rang, the cheerful man at the other end introduced himself as Richard Branson. I couldn't believe it. The multi-millionaire chairman of the Virgin empire was talking to me!

'Are the reports I'm reading true that your son Ashley's only hope is to go to New York for a lifesaving operation?'

'Yes,' I said. I was almost struck speechless in awe of this man.

'And what about the cost?'

'Most of it's come in.'

'How are you getting there?' he asked.

'Well, thanks to the generosity of your company, Ashley already has a complimentary ticket.'

'What about you and your wife?'

'We're paying for our own tickets,' I replied.

'Don't worry. They're already paid for,' Richard Branson said. 'You'll all be travelling on Virgin Atlantic at my expense.'

'Thank you very much.' A wave of relief swept over me.

He gave me his personal phone number and said: 'If you need anything at all give me a ring.'

On the other side of the Atlantic Dr Fred Epstein was also kept busy with reporters. He talked to them about brain-stem tumours like Ashley's: 'In the UK there are only three or four each year. Because I have had a particular interest in this part of the nervous system I operate on thirty or forty a year. If the operation is successful it could enhance and prolong Ashley's life indefinitely.'

In between packing suitcases, we had more phone calls and interviews with the Press. The media people didn't seem to believe in having weekends off.

One woman reporter from BBC Radio Kent tried her best to get Ashley to make a comment on the forthcoming trip to New York. As usual, he remained tight-lipped and highly suspicious. Finally, in exaspera-tion she gave up and turned to walk away.

'Daddy, are we *really* going on a big, big plane?' Ashley asked.

The reporter turned on her heels and raced back, tape recorder once more at the ready.

'Will you say that into the microphone, please, Ashley?'

'No!' was his blunt reply.

Later that day, Sue rang to say that they had closed the phone lines on the 'Ashley to America' appeal. So much money had come in that they were actually turning it away! A staggering total of £70,000 had been raised—about $113,000. The people on the hotline were suggesting instead that people give money to other charities helping sick children.

By now we were totally exhausted. But we were also overwhelmed by people's generosity for a little boy they didn't even know. I heard some wonderful stories about how the money was given. One policeman from Sussex was out on motor patrol with a colleague.

'We got called out to a drunk and disorderly man,' he recounted. 'There I was, wrestling and tussling with this drunken man, trying to get him into the patrol car. In the middle of all that a little old lady came rushing up to me and shoved a £10 note in my hand.

' "Here, quick," she said, urgency rising in her voice. "You've got to get this to that policeman in Kent." '

As a result, the policeman put in £5 of his own money, 'just for good luck,' he told me.

One man phoned Fred Epstein from his prison cell in Saudi Arabia and offered to give a substantial sum of money to the appeal. 'The problem is, I need to get out first so I can go to the bank,' he said. 'Can you use your influence to get me out?' Despite his willingness to help, he wasn't allowed out of his cell!

A man living on the streets in the Midlands walked into his local police station and dumped a bag on the counter. 'Here, this is for that Kent policeman's kid,' he said, and walked out. Inside was cash totalling £500.

A Greek businessman put £5,000 straight into Fred Epstein's account for Ashley's operation. A businessman flying the Atlantic pledged £1,000 by phone. Several children donated 50p or so from their pocket money. A Londoner deposited $5,000 in a New York bank. Another man ran the New York Marathon and donated his sponsor money to Ashley.

For the previous couple of weeks people in our church, Gravesend Christian Fellowship, had been praying and fasting for Ashley's recovery. They had decided to set aside three Tuesdays when the whole church would pray for Ashley. There would be a prayer meeting at six in the morning, another at lunchtime and a third one in the early evening.

The church people kept giving us words of encouragement. One person said: 'God's going to perform a miracle in healing Ashley, and his testimony will be a well publicized and documented one.' That second part was certainly proving true now.

On Sunday, 30 October, Vivien, Sue Roberton and I, together with little Ashley, travelled to Heathrow ready to fly to New York courtesy of Virgin Atlantic. The Civil Aviation Authority had given us immediate clearance through the airport. We had really wanted to take Simon and Michelle along with us, but we were only going to be away for four weeks at the most and the children were being taken care of by my sister, Angie. The people from Police Welfare had also agreed to keep a watchful eye on them.

For our journey from our home in Northfleet, Kent, to Heathrow, our 'taxi driver' was Kent Police Federation chairperson Inspector Jan Berry. As a mere constable I learned early on in my police career that inspectors needed to be treated with great respect. I'd always offer to carry the inspector's bags whenever I could. Today was the first and only time that an inspector carried my bags for *me!*

The Press were waiting to talk to us at Heathrow. There seemed to be no escape from them. At the Press conference Jan Berry said about the fundraising effort: 'It restored our faith in human nature. The appeal brought out the best in people rather than the worst, which we as police officers see all too often. The response was amazing.'

I told them our hopes were rising that the forthcoming operation in New York could save Ashley's life. 'On behalf of my family I would like to say how overwhelmed we have been by people's generosity,' I said. I really meant it.

After the Press conference the four of us—Sue was

coming along to give us support and to ward off the Press—were escorted to the plane by the Virgin representative. Soon we had taken off and were on our way to New York.

As we travelled over the Atlantic, Ashley's story was being broadcast on Sky News. Each seat had its own three-inch colour TV screen on the back of the seat in front. Passengers could watch one of the videos being shown or else tune in to live satellite TV. I noticed an old lady sitting level with us in the middle aisle. This old lady stared at Ashley, then at the pictures on satellite TV. Surprise came on her face as she recognized him. Then, without a word, she disappeared.

An hour or so later, she came up to us with a plastic bag full of money of every currency imaginable. 'This is for Ashley's appeal,' she said. When we counted it, we found that it totalled about $700 (£430). She had gone up and down the plane asking for donations from both passengers and cabin staff.

The crew on board were extremely helpful. One cabin crew member, Nicos, a blond Greek man in his twenties, really took to Ashley. He showed him around the plane and the two of them drew pictures for the captain. Then Nicos took Ashley up the spiral staircase in the first class section to meet the captain and crew. We were invited to join them.

In the cockpit we met the crew. The space wasn't much bigger than the inside of my car, yet it had to hold four people. The captain invited Ashley to sit in his seat, but he refused.

'I want to go. It's boring,' he said to me.

I was staggered. 'How could you *possibly* be bored in the cockpit of a 747 jumbo jet?' I asked him. I was finding it all fascinating. In fact, I think I would have sat in the captain's seat, given half the chance.

After the visit to the cockpit, Sue Roberton had a word with me. 'Look, Nicos wants to give Ashley the crucifix he always wears around his neck. I think he'll be offended if you don't accept it.'

It was a valuable gold crucifix on a heavy gold chain, probably a family heirloom. Shortly before we landed in New York, Nicos just took it off his neck and put it on Ashley. My son wore it until his operation. Because it's so valuable, Vivien is now wearing it until Ashley is old enough to take care of it.

The plane landed at J F Kennedy Airport, New York, at five o'clock in the evening. We went through immigration with ease. The Virgin representative, a young American woman, took care of things for us. But once we got out into the airport building itself we were told no one was being let in or out of the airport because of a bomb scare. The nightmare of New York seemed to be upon us.

Just when things were looking really bad, the representative showed us out through the tradespeople's entrance.

When we got out to the front of the airport we discovered that the Kent Police Benevolent Fund had kindly ordered a stretch limousine to take us from the airport to New York itself. The limousine was complete with TV, drinks cabinet and ice—virtually a hotel on wheels. The trouble was, we were so exhausted after three days of dealing with the Press and a long flight that we couldn't really appreciate our luxurious ride into New York.

As we crossed the bridge to Manhattan Island, which forms New York itself, I looked ahead and saw the gloomy, darkening skyline of an autumn New York. It brought to my mind a futuristic film I once saw, *Escape from New York*, in which crime had risen by 400 per cent and the whole of Manhattan Island now served as a prison, enclosed by high walls.

A plane carrying the President of the US, played in the film by Donald Pleasence, had crash-landed in New York. The president was being held by the brutal inmates, who called themselves the National Liberation Front of America.

A renowned villain, Snake Plissken (Kurt Russell),

was sent by the authorities into the city to bring the president out—dead or alive. Implanted in an artery on each side of the villain's brain was a capsule the size of a ball-point pen tip. These capsules contained a timing device that would explode if he didn't completed his mission within twenty-two hours.

As we crossed the bridge to the island, New York was just how I imagined it from the film. As the darkness descended over the skyscraper city, I thought of what a scary place this was. Here I was, taking my wife and youngest son to a strange place in strange surroundings, 3,000 miles from home. And now I must trust my precious son's entire life into the hands of a man I had never met.

Like the rescuer in the film, Ashley in a sense had an explosive timing device in his brain. If Dr Epstein couldn't operate to remove it here in New York, there was little hope for Ashley's future.

Time was running out, and I knew Ashley might not survive to reach his fifth birthday.

11 Miracle on 34th Street?

The stretch limousine carrying Andrew, Vivien, Ashley and Sue Roberton got caught in a huge delay in rush-hour traffic. New York is one of the busiest cities in the world, and a traffic hold-up can last for hours.

Eventually they arrived at Ronald McDonald House, New York, where they had arranged to stay.

Once they had struggled inside with their luggage as well as Ashley in his pushchair, they went to the reception desk. They had heard a lot about American hospitality, but were surprised and a little hurt when the woman at the reception desk simply said: 'Sit down over there and someone will be along in a minute.' She hardly said hello, and didn't seem very interested in them.

They sat in the reception area for over half an hour waiting for someone to show them around and then take them to their room. They weren't even offered a cup of coffee. After all the attention of the media during the last few days, Andrew and Vivien felt suddenly alone and very afraid for Ashley's future.

When eventually they got to their own rooms they discovered they had to make their own meals—and they had nothing to eat or drink for breakfast the next morning. They had heard there was an all-night superstore nearby, and while Andrew stayed with Ashley in the room, Vivien and Sue went out and bought tea, coffee, bread, milk and other basics.

By the time they got back, it was 10.30pm and they were shattered beyond belief. That wasn't surprising. It was now 3.30a.m. English time and Andrew and Vivien had been on the move since 6.30 the previous morning. They hadn't slept on the plane, and now all they could think about was sleep.

Sue was so tired she didn't know what to do with herself.

'I can't wait to collapse into bed,' she said, dramatically throwing back the cover on the bed in her room. 'Oh, no! I can't believe it!' she suddenly shouted. 'After all this travelling I've got to make my own bed!'

Vivien couldn't help laughing at Sue's little outburst. But Sue was right. The policy at the house was that all guests had to make their own beds. That even applied to guests who had just travelled the Atlantic and had been up for more than twenty hours without sleep. They were paying only $20 a night and were expected to take a small share in the running of the house.

Three hours later, Andrew and Vivien were awake again. Although it was only the small hours of the morning, their minds weren't used to the time difference. It took ages for them to get back to sleep again.

Monday, 31 October 1994 dawned. They were all up early to make their breakfast and get ready for their first meeting with Dr Fred Epstein.

As it was so early, they decided to walk to his office on East 34th Street. It was a walk of three-quarters of an hour from the house on East 73rd, along First Avenue, to Epstein's office, which was situated between First and Second Avenues.

It was a cold but pleasant late autumn day. The streets were full of people rushing to work or to the big department stores. They passed the huge United Nations building and saw in the distance the distinct, pointed roof of the Chrysler Building and the famous Empire State Building, which had featured in many movies, most notably *King Kong* and *Sleepless in Seattle*.

Talking of movies, Andrew and Vivien had often seen the steaming drains of New York City on the big screen but thought it was just an idea of the special effects departments. As they weaved their way through the busyness of First Avenue that day, they noticed with amazement that steaming drains really *were* a part of the city's life. They discovered that steam was used to heat many of the skyscrapers and other buildings. The excess steam was piped off into the drains.

They stopped for Andrew to take a picture of Vivien and Sue beside one of the steaming drains pretending to choke on the fumes. Sometimes the drains really *did* smell, though not usually.

As they walked along First Avenue towards Dr Epstein's office on 34th Street, they saw a billboard outside a movie theatre advertising the brand new remake of the classic Christmas film *Miracle on 34th Street*, starring Richard Attenborough.

'That's what Ashley needs—a miracle,' thought Andrew. And that new miracle on 34th Street, he hoped, would be performed not by Santa Claus in a department store but by another white-haired man, Fred Epstein, in an operating theatre.

Dr Epstein's office was in a modern office block typical of New York. They walked into the lobby through glass doors. The lobby was narrow with a surveillance monitor directly in front of them as they entered. They watched themselves on the monitor as they moved through the lobby, then spoke to the security guard, who also served as the bell boy.

'We've come here to see Dr Epstein.'

'Ah, yes. You need the 10th floor.'

He pressed the button and they waited until the elevator arrived. It was smaller than they expected and they had to squeeze into it with Ashley in his pushchair.

They emerged into a corridor on the tenth floor. At the far end of the corridor there was a glass door with another panelled glass door to the right. Here they rang the bell and the receptionist inside pressed a button to open the lock.

The office they entered was pleasantly decorated in a modern style. The floor was covered in a red-and-black carpet with wavy patterns on it. There were several black-framed chairs with red upholstery. The desk where the receptionist sat was also black, its front stretching down to the floor. It was positioned directly opposite the door.

'Hi. May I help you?' the receptionist asked pleasantly.

'Yes. Mr and Mrs Fowle and Sue Roberton with Ashley,' Vivien said. 'We've come to see Dr Epstein.'

'Yes, of course. Now, Dr Epstein has telephoned to say he's going to be a little late for the appointment.'

'That suits us,' said Andrew. 'We're early and I'm feeling hungry. Is there anywhere we can get something to eat?'

She disappeared for a moment and returned with a black lady who had long Afro-Caribbean hair. She introduced herself as Vivien from England.

'Another Vivien from England. I feel at home!' said Vivien Fowle.

'Now, I hear you're hungry. I can recommend the Gemini Diner. It's just round the corner. I'll come down and point the way for you, if you'd like.'

She went with them back down the small elevator and out onto the street. The Gemini Diner was on the corner of Second Avenue and 35th Street, a short walk away.

Once in the Gemini Diner, they placed their orders. Andrew asked for a steak sandwich thinking that, just like in England, he would get a small piece of meat between two slices of bread. Instead, he was absolutely shocked to be served with a 16oz steak on a large sesame seed bun, a huge pile of French fries—enough for two people—and, separately, a large bowl of salad big enough to feed a family of five. It was his first taste of American food—and as a result of it, he put on 28lb in weight during their stay in New York.

Back in the office, the receptionist told them to take a seat. There was a black door next to the reception desk that led to the toilets. On the other side of the desk there was an archway that led to the seating area. Here they sat with Ashley on their laps. A few other people were also seated there. There was a water machine nearby with conical paper cups just like Andrew and Vivien had seen in American movies.

Leading off from this area were two consulting rooms, one of which was Dr Epstein's. Soon a woman came out from Dr Epstein's office and introduced herself.

'Hi. My name's JoAnn Baldwin, I'm Dr Epstein's office manager.'

Vivien stared back. There was something familiar about this woman. When Vivien had spoken on the phone to someone from Dr Epstein's office she had pictured the woman's face, and this was that same person.

'Excuse me, are you Dr Epstein's secretary?' Vivien asked.

'No,' she replied. 'But I believe I've spoken to you on the telephone.'

This time it was Andrew's turn for a surprise. He had spoken to JoAnn several times on the phone, but this was their first meeting. She was the opposite in appearance to how he had imagined her. He had pictured a tall, slim brunette. Instead she was like Lisa Minelli—big eyes, short, with dark hair in a bob.

She was friendly and welcoming and showed them into Fred Epstein's office, where they sat down on a large three-seater settee to wait for him. His office was very light and airy. He had see-through brown blinds that were partly pulled down. They could see out across the city, with its skyscrapers dominating the view. Unlike last night, those skyscrapers didn't look at all sinister or threatening.

As they looked around Dr Epstein's office they noticed several personal touches. He had a range of model cars on his shelf, one-twelfth actual size. They included a modern Ferrari and some vintage cars. On the walls he had lots of photographs of himself, his wife Kathy and his five children ranging in age from four to twenty-two. It was obvious that he was a family man. There were also several photographs with sporting themes. In one there was a yacht with the sails billowing out in 3-D.

They also noticed on the walls several *Reader's Digest* articles mounted in frames. These included the first one Vivien had read and another from January 1983 called 'The Transformation of Aaron Alligator', which was about Dr Epstein's first successful operation on a brain-stem tumour. As soon as they saw the articles they nudged each other.

'It doesn't look like he's embarrassed about those articles,' Andrew remarked quietly. 'If he was, why would he have them framed on his office wall?'

They sat for a few minutes waiting, and then the great man walked in. He was over six feet tall, slim, with white hair greying at the temples and a broad grin in an open, friendly face. Although he was obviously well into his fifties, he looked much younger, with boyish looks and fun in his sparkling eyes.

Vivien thought he was just like a mad professor. He wore expensive-looking cowboy boots (she later found them for sale at 'only' $2,000) and an old-fashioned suit that didn't fit him. It was so old it looked like a $2 reject from the Salvation Army. He almost had the looks of Charlton Heston to go with the voice that they had heard several times on the phone.

'Hi, I'm Dr Epstein.'

'Hello. Andrew Fowle, my wife Vivien and Sue Roberton from the Police Welfare.'

'Hi.'

'And this is Ashley.'

'Hi, Ashley. I'm pleased to meet you.'

Ashley shrank back and didn't reply. By now he was so wary of doctors that he didn't trust any of them. To Ashley, Dr Epstein was just another doctor, another series of tests or another form of treatment.

Andrew and Vivien were in awe of this man because they had travelled all that way knowing he could be the one actually to save Ashley's life.

'How was your trip over?' he asked matter-of-factly.

'Great. We're very tired, though.'

'Dr Epstein, can I ask a question?' said Vivien suddenly.

'Sure.'

'Those articles on the wall. Are you embarrassed by them?'

117

'No, why should I be? I wrote them.'

'But we were told you found them embarrassing.'

'Who told you that?'

'Dr Joan Whitehead at Guy's Hospital in London.'

'Guy's Hospital? I've never heard of it. Now, getting to the business in hand, I want you to look at these.' He showed them Ashley's scans, clipping them on a series of light-boxes fixed to the wall. 'As I said on the phone, I can tell just from looking at these scans that Ashley's tumour is benign.'

'You mean it's not cancer.'

'No, it's not. Now, what treatment has he had so far?'

'He finished radiotherapy in June.'

'I can tell by the way Ashley looks that he's on steroids. He's what we call Cushingoid in appearance. That means his face and neck are swollen. What dose is he on?'

They told him. Dr Epstein then explained the various steps he planned to take during the operation. 'I intend to debulk the tumour,' he continued.

'What does that mean exactly?'

'It means to reduce the tumour's size. I do this by coring it from the inside out, a bit like coring an apple.'

'Right.'

'I've told you what I'm going to do. Now you're going to ask me these questions: "What is the risk?" and: "How long will the operation take?" '

'That's right!' said Andrew. 'But how did you know?'

'All the parents I meet want to know the answer to those questions. So, I'll give you my answers. First the risk. This is a very hazardous operation. Ashley has an 80 per cent chance of surviving through it, though I don't know the long-term prospects. But then, there's a risk with any operation, especially in this type where we're operating on the brain and spinal cord. Without this surgery his fate is sealed. He won't survive for longer than six to twelve months.'

'That short a time?'

'Yes, indeed. I need to say as well that because of the steroids and the radiotherapy, he's a very fragile little boy.

Ashley's condition is very precarious because he's got weakness in his arms and legs, has difficulty breathing and is overweight from taking the steroids. That makes the risk greater than normal.'

'OK, so how long will the surgery take?'

'It'll last about seven or eight hours, possibly longer.'

'As long as that?'

'Yes, I'm afraid so. So you'll have to find something to keep yourselves busy while it's going on.'

They talked about money. Because Andrew and Vivien didn't have American health insurance, they were liable to pay privately for the operation and hospital stay. Fred Epstein knew this and offered to waive the fee.

'No, thanks,' said Andrew. 'We've managed to raise all the money from generous people in England. It's already in the hospital bank account.'

'OK.'

Suddenly, four-year-old Ashley spoke up. 'I don't like you,' he said, looking directly at Dr Epstein. Vivien felt like crawling under the table.

'Why's that, Ashley?' asked Fred Epstein, beaming a smile at the little boy.

"Cos you've got white hair.'

They all burst out laughing. Ashley had said that before about Andrew's assistant commissioner at work. At least he was beginning to talk to the man who could save his life.

'You know something, Dr Epstein?' asked Vivien suddenly.

'What's that, ma'am?'

'God's chosen you to do this operation on my son.'

'I know,' said Fred Epstein, simply and with deep meaning.

The meeting lasted about an hour. After it was all over, Andrew and Vivien wanted to phone relatives in England.

'Feel free to use my phone here,' said Dr Epstein with a casual shrug of his shoulders. 'I'll go away and make myself scarce.' It was as if they were phoning someone down the road instead of 3,000 miles away on the other side of the Atlantic.

Fred Epstein left the room and they phoned a couple of people.

After the meeting they went to the hospital to book in. They walked down 34th Street, turned into First Avenue and the hospital was a short walk along on the left-hand side. It was a sprawling series of buildings stretching all the way to 24th Street.

New York University Medical Centre was popularly known as 'NYU' or by its old name 'Tische Hospital'. They got to it by walking on the sidewalk up a long in-out driveway that served as a kind of taxi rank. The building they entered was large and multi-storeyed with a huge entrance. Parts of the outside were a bit like a dilapidated British National Health Service hospital, though it was one of the largest and best medical centres in the world, with ultra-modern equipment inside.

The reception area was glass-fronted with revolving doors moving constantly. To each side were two other sets of double doors. The inside was huge, like the reception hall of a museum. There was a large marble reception desk about ten metres long where the security guards stood. To the right was a pharmacy and a general shop. To the left was a square arch through which they went to another large reception hall.

Here Andrew, Vivien and Sue went to a desk, introduced themselves and were told to take a seat with Ashley. After about half an hour they were called into a small office where a woman took down all their details—name, address, patient's date of birth, family doctor.

Then she asked: 'Do you have a health insurance number?'

They didn't.

'So, how are you going to pay for this?'

'The money should already be in the hospital account. We had it sent over from England by electronic transfer.'

She went away and checked. A few minutes later she came back.

'It isn't in the account,' she said.

'Well, the instructions were definitely faxed through,' Andrew said. He gave the name of the person who had accepted the money. Once more she disappeared to check.

'Yes, that's all in order,' she said on her return.

Andrew and Vivien had to sign all the relevant forms. Only then were they allowed to take Ashley in his pushchair up to the ward, Nine West.

They used the elevator to get to the ninth floor. Nine West, they discovered, was an old, run-down series of rooms. Half of it had been partitioned off for refurbishment. Plastic sheets had been used to keep the dust out of the half that was still in use.

The room Ashley was to stay in had four beds. He was in the bed nearest the window. In between the beds was a section with a sink and a sluice. There was a TV already in the room but they had to pay $5 a day if they wanted it connected.

When they arrived on the ward all Ashley's name tags were in pink because in the US Ashley was generally a girl's name. Like Dr Epstein in his initial phone call, the hospital staff assumed Ashley to be a girl. Even on TV, when he was explaining the operation, Dr Epstein called Ashley 'she'.

Meanwhile, over in England, the Press had made another mistake that was causing a furore. Somehow, Jonathan Mayo, a spokesman for Dr Epstein, announced to the Press that Fred Epstein was waiving his fee for the operation. This caused a flood of phone calls to the Kent police headquarters demanding to know what had happened to the money that members of the public had so sacrificially donated.

The following day the announcement was corrected. Apparently it was based on a misunderstanding on Fred Epstein's part. Jonathan Mayo said: 'Dr Epstein offered to waive the fee but because the community had raised enough money, the waiving of the fee was not necessary.'

Back on Nine West, the hospital staff did some routine blood tests on Ashley. While they were drawing the sample Andrew said: 'If Ashley needs a blood transfusion during his operation, I'd like him to have some of my blood. I'm O positive, the same blood group as he is.'

'I'm sorry,' the nurse replied. 'It's too late. If we'd known before, we could have arranged it. You would have needed to have come in a few days ago so your blood could be screened to make sure it was acceptable.'

Andrew had heard that some hospitals in the US weren't too fussy about where they got their blood supplies from. But the nurse assured him that all their blood was screened and there was no chance of Ashley getting HIV or hepatitis B.

After taking blood, they had to put a line into one of Ashley's veins. This had always been the most difficult task of all. First, Ashley hated it and would scream the place down. In England they had at first tried using a cream containing lignocaine that was supposed to anaesthetize the skin, making it less painful when the needle was inserted. It took at least half an hour for the cream to work. Even then, the needle would hurt worse than a bee sting. Ashley got to the point where he would scream as soon as they put the cream on. Then they had to learn how to distract him and suddenly insert the needle.

The second problem was that, after all the tests and operations over the four years of Ashley's life, he was like a pin cushion. Many of his veins had collapsed or couldn't be found. The medical staff used a strap on his arm and even tapped the back of his hand to make his veins there more prominent. Nothing seemed to work.

In the end they connected a line to a vein in his foot. It was right over the foot joint and they had to use a splint to hold his foot in place. Otherwise, every time he moved his foot, the line would come out.

Andrew stayed in the room with Ashley that first night while Vivien and Sue went back to Ronald

McDonald House. The seat-bed Andrew slept in was like a wooden armchair that folded down flat. Underneath was a drawer with a cushion in it. Andrew had to pull out the drawer, take the cushion and put it on the open drawer. Although it was a fairly primitive bed, Andrew found it reasonably comfortable.

At six the following morning Ashley was given a premedication injection to sedate him. Vivien and Sue arrived a short while later and Ashley was wheeled to the operating theatre.

Little Ashley was very nervous about the operation. 'Ashley is quite overwhelmed by it,' Vivien told the Press a few minutes later. 'He doesn't really understand about the operation. We've kept a lot of it from him, but he doesn't really like the idea. I told him he would be asleep. He's quite happy in himself.'

Andrew recalls:
We went along the corridor together to the operating theatre—me, Vivien, Sue and Ashley.

Although Ashley was only semi-conscious because of the premedication, he was sitting up on the trolley like a little Buddha. There's a photo of him sitting there waiting to go in. He has puffy cheeks and he looks really miserable.

The hospital staff wanted one of us to go into the operating theatre with him while he was being anaesthetized. Vivien couldn't face it and stayed in the corridor. So it was down to me.

As Ashley sat on the trolley, the hospital staff dressed me up in a blue gown, covered my feet with special protective slippers and put a face mask on me. I guess I must have looked like one of the surgeons. Once I was dressed up, I could go in with Ashley.

Soon I was in the operating theatre itself. Unlike hospitals in Britain, there was no anteroom. This was the very place where the big operation would take place in a few minutes' time.

When Ashley was lying down on my lap, the anaesthetist first flushed out the line to make sure there were no impurities in it. Then he slowly introduced the anaesthetic itself. As it began to take hold, Ashley's eyelids fluttered, then closed completely. Ashley was out cold.

Panic overtook me. Even at this late hour, 3,000 miles from home, I was having second thoughts. Were we doing the right thing? Would we spend the rest of our lives regretting this moment?

Then I remembered. We were here because God had helped us. It couldn't have been anyone else. And surely he wouldn't let us down now?

Still, I couldn't shake the doubts. Ashley, my little son, was lying there as still as death. Would he ever wake up again?

I had this vision of Dr Epstein, sometime in the next few hours coming out of the operating theatre, pulling off his mask and shaking his head. 'I'm sorry, sir, ma'am. We've lost him,' he would say.

I bent down over Ashley's prostrate form and kissed his warm cheek.

'Goodbye, Ashley,' I whispered with finality, tears coursing down my cheeks. 'Goodbye, son.'

Then I turned and without a glance back I walked out of the doors of the operating theatre.

12 *Eureka!*

As soon as Andrew had left the operating theatre, Dr Fred Epstein's nine-strong team, including theatre staff, computer operators and laser experts, all got to work. Fred Epstein himself would not come into the operating theatre until much later, when the preliminary stages were over.

They were all experienced at this kind of operation and knew they were in for another very long day. The room was packed with the vast amounts of modern equipment needed for such delicate surgery. In addition to the traditional operating table, anaesthetic pump and trays of instruments, there was a vast, seven-foot operating microscope. There were also monitors, lasers to vaporize tissue, drills and a Cavitron, the unique pencil-shaped instrument developed specially to debulk brain-stem and spinal-cord tumours.

The nurses unwrapped long-handled micro-surgical instruments and placed them on a movable overhead table. The instruments had to be laid out in exactly the right order for the surgeons to use them. In addition to special scissors, nerve hooks, retractors and suction irrigators, there was a special pair of forceps with a flat tip. Fred had designed them to pull back the membranes and expose the tumour itself without harming surrounding nerve tissue. They were nicknamed 'Fred's Ferrari' because they were sleek and supple, just like Fred's red sports car of the same name.

Everything was in its place ready for Ashley's operation. Ashley was now under a general anaesthetic. A mask was placed over his face and he was given halothane, a gas that made reversal of the anaesthesia more rapid than conventional gas. With this type of operation it was important to be able to bring the patient back to consciousness quickly.

Once Ashley was safely under the influence of the gas, the anaesthetist Murray Canter attached a pulsoximeter to Ashley's big toe in order to measure the amount of oxygen in his blood. He also put electrocardiogram leads to Ashley's chest to monitor his heart activity.

Opening Ashley's mouth, Murray inserted a plastic breathing-tube and attached it to a respirator. He connected the line already in Ashley's foot to a monitor in order to measure his blood gases. He also injected a muscle relaxant to paralyze Ashley's internal muscles. From now until the end of the operation, Ashley would be dependent on machines to do his breathing for him.

While Murray Canter worked, another doctor taped Ashley's eyes shut to prevent them from drying out. He also inserted a catheter to drain and monitor urine output.

Gently, the theatre staff rolled Ashley onto his stomach, making sure that the various tubes and wires stayed in place. The operating table was already covered in a warm blanket and a foam cushion. Pads were placed under his chest and shoulders so he could breathe easily. His head was then raised onto a three-pronged headrest and fixed in position.

Next, Ashley's hair needed to be shaved. Fred Epstein knew how much appearance mattered to children. He always insisted to his team that only as much hair as was necessary was shaved off. In Ashley's case the doctor shaved the soft downy hair from his shoulders up to the nape of his neck. From there the shaving continued up about three inches through his curly, blond hair to the *inion,* the widest point of his skull at the back. After the loose hair had been cleared, the remaining hair near the shaved part was slicked down with petroleum jelly to keep it out of the way and to prevent infection.

Then came the all-important cleaning process. For ten whole minutes an area of skin from Ashley's lower skull down to his shoulders was swabbed time and again with a powerful antiseptic. Once the area had been draped with a blue cloth and a plastic drape, the first phase of the actual operation could begin. By now two hours had passed.

It was time for Rick Abbott, Fred Epstein's partner, to go to work. The provisional diagnosis he had been given by Fred was that Ashley had an 'intraaxial cervicomedullary tumour extending from the medulla to about the first thoracic vertebra'. That was the area that must be opened up.

Grasping a scalpel Rick made a clean, straight incision from the most prominent part of Ashley's head right down his neck.

Using the Bovie, a metal instrument that sends out a low voltage, Rick then separated the muscles from the spine and lower skull. The Bovie could burn off tissue or close off blood vessels as necessary. He used a retractor to hold the area open and expose the bone.

Before him he could see the lower part of Ashley's skull and the bones of his neck.

Next he opened the lower section of Ashley's skull using a procedure known as *suboccipital craniotomy*. Rick Abbott used a perforator—a stainless steel surgical air-drill—to make a circle of tiny holes half an inch in diameter. Then with a ronguer, a tiny pair of pliers, he chipped away at the bone between the holes.

Then he turned his attention to Ashley's neck. 'Midas Rex, please,' Rick Abbott said suddenly. The Midas Rex was a compact pneumatic drill that looked like a thick pencil with a wire attached. With its 60,000 revolutions per minute it could cut through bone like butter. Using it, Rick did a *laminectomy*. First, he made an incision along the full length of each side of Ashley's neck bones, severing a portion of the spine. Then he separated the ligaments beneath the bone from the dura covering the spinal cord itself.

Carefully, he lifted the three-inch section of spine in one piece and handed it to a nurse, who placed it in a basin filled with saline solution.

Eventually, the dura, the toughest of the three meninges (membranes) surrounding Ashley's brain stem and spinal cord, was exposed fully to view. Now was the time to wheel the huge, unwieldy operating microscope into position. Once it was ready, it was time to cut into the dura itself. Rick took a deep breath and began.

It was a long section to work on, right from Ashley's skull down his neck to his shoulders, but Rick worked quickly. As each piece of dura was folded back it was held into position by a single stitch and covered in a special gauze to prevent it shrinking and making closure difficult.

At last the dura was opened. Now the operating staff could clearly see the cerebellar tonsils, the lower brain stem and the cervical spinal cord, pulsating to Ashley's rhythmic heartbeat. It didn't take the most expert neurosurgeon to see that there was something seriously wrong with Ashley's nervous system. The spinal cord was bulging where it should have been level.

Now it was time to bring in Fred Epstein for the most difficult part of the operation. One of the nurses went to the phone. 'Hi, JoAnn. Tell Fred we need him down here.'

A few minutes later the doors swung open dramatically and Fred walked in, dressed in a blue gown and wearing his favourite green clogs. A nurse helped him into a pair of sterile gloves and he walked over to where Ashley lay on the operating table.

'Now, what have we got here?' he asked unnecessarily, peering through the microscope.

During his training to be a doctor, Fred Epstein had wanted to be a psychiatrist, like his father. Then for a month he watched a neurosurgeon at work, and decided to switch.

Joe Ransohoff MD, who at that time was the chairman of the Neurosurgery Department at New York University, had cautioned him. 'Being a brain surgeon isn't like being a shrink,' he said. 'A shrink just thinks he's inside the patient's head, but a brain surgeon really is. It can be pretty scary in there, too.'

Fred wasn't put off and was eventually appointed director of the newly formed division of paediatric neurosurgery in 1985. Now he was about to go inside another very young patient's head, and he knew that it would indeed be a pretty scary place to be for the next two or three hours.

'Ultrasound,' Fred said suddenly.

A nurse handed him a tiny transducer that he placed on Ashley's brain stem and then on the lowest part of his exposed spinal cord. Looking at the monitor he gauged the extent of the tumour. Ultrasound had revolutionized neurosurgery in the previous ten years or so. Just as ultrasound could trace the size and growth of a baby in the womb, so it could trace and measure a tumour on the brain stem or spinal cord.

Once the extent of Ashley's tumour was checked against the MRI scans, Fred Epstein put a stimulating electrode on the brain stem. This would be used to give 'evoked potentials'—signals of electrical activity in the brain. If the signals changed by even a fraction, it would indicate that Fred was coming too close to normal healthy tissue and would need to stop before any damage was done.

Using the microscope, Fred Epstein studied the tumour as it merged with the nervous tissue, much like the marbling in a steak.

'OK,' Fred said in his customary pep-talk to his team. 'This is a four-year-old boy from England called Ashley. His parents have had to raise a lot of money to bring him over here. He's cute and he's blond and the Press just love him. Let's make sure he goes back to England looking good so I look good, too.'

Laughter filled the room. Then there was a slight pause as the team once more realized that this was not just a technical skill they were performing; they were working to save the life of a real, desperately ill child.

'OK, laser, please,' Fred Epstein said. The power was switched on and he took up a small, wand-shaped instrument and began. The laser Fred used made an incision as it went along, much as a magnifying glass burns a hole in a piece of paper when the sun's rays are focused through it. The incision, known as a *myelotomy,* was made along the spinal cord covering the full length of the tumour.

Fred Epstein opened the incision further using bayonet forceps and tied the tissue back, exposing the full extent of the tumour. The grey of the tumour, which Fred often described as 'the enemy', contrasted sharply with the healthy white of the brain-stem and spinal-cord tissue. As he had thought before the operation, it appeared to be a low-grade astrocytoma and was fairly distinct from adjacent normal nerve tissue.

Fred went back to the tumour's widest point and made another incision, carefully removing a section of the tumour for laboratory analysis. By now a TV crew from England had set up their cameras and would later show this part of the operation across the UK.

As Fred held the severed piece of tumour in a pair of forceps, he carefully examined it in 3-D through the two eyepieces of the operating microscope. What he saw confirmed in his own thinking what he had guessed when he first studied Ashley's scans.

'All I held in my hand was living tumour,' he said later. The truth was that the radiotherapy Ashley had been through in England had done nothing to destroy the tumour cells. Fred himself had once said: 'Radiation isn't for very young children.' It was a controversial statement to make, even in his own country.

Now it was time to use the Cavitron to debulk the rest of Ashley's tumour. The Cavitron had originally been developed as a dental descaler in the 1950s. Ultrasonic waves travel through a hollow tube and over a series of parallel metal plates in the handle. These plates resonate with the high-pitched sound waves causing the metal tip to vibrate. The basic Cavitron removes plaque, while a separate aspirator is used to suck up the resulting tartar. A more advanced Cavitron, still not widely used under the British National Health Service, has an aspirator built into the tip so that the dentist can use it singlehanded.

The Cavitron ultrasonic surgical aspirator was developed by Fred Epstein's mentor Joe Ransohoff in the 1970s specifically for brain tumours. It was designed by researchers at the New York University Medical Centre and the Cavitron Corporation, now Valley Lab in Boulder, Colorado. The tip vibrates 23,000 times a second, literally turning the tumour tissue to liquid and then sucking it out through its hollow tip.

Using the Cavitron on a brain tumour was one thing; using it on a brain-stem and spinal-cord tumour such as Ashley's was a very different kettle of fish. The area was considered much too small even for the surgical Cavitron, so until a few years ago no one had attempted it.

Thirteen years ago Fred Epstein had been sitting in the dentist's chair, the dentist hovering over him with a dental Cavitron. Suddenly, Fred saw in his mind's eye the surgical Cavitron being used to vaporize a spinal cord tumour, little by little, and suctioning it.

Archimedes had leapt out of the bath with a cry of 'Eureka!' Now Fred leapt out of the dentist's chair, knocking over a tray of instruments. Apologizing to the dentist, he hurried downstairs and out onto the street. In the cab on the way to the hospital his idea began to crystallize. 'It's so simple,' he murmured.

'Are you talking to me, buddy?' the driver asked.

Later, as he explained his suggestion to his boss, Joe Ransohoff, the senior surgeon struck a note of caution about the potential for damage to the spinal cord.

Fred sprang to his own defence. 'We'd be going for cure, not just tumour management until the kid died,' he said.

'Fantastic,' Ransohoff said after thinking for a minute or two. 'Do it.'

Fred's first operation on a spinal cord tumour using the Cavitron was a success. Steven Benson's story was written up in *Reader's Digest* under the title 'The Transformation of Aaron Alligator', after Steven's favourite character in a Dr Seuss book.

Now Fred was using that same adapted instrument to debulk Ashley's tumour. Alternating between the laser and the Cavitron, Fred Epstein worked along the whole length of the tumour, removing miniscule amounts at a time. With the part of the tumour in the brain stem, it was rather like coring an apple and then working from the inside out. As he reached the spinal cord, it was more like removing the lead of a pencil. It was a long, slow process and it involved extreme care. One slip and Ashley would die or be permanently paralyzed.

Fred Epstein had to resist his natural instinct to move quickly, exposing and destroying yet more tumour. 'Be very careful. Easy now,' he mumbled to himself. His colleagues were used to such nervous chatter and ignored it.

As he progressed, Fred Epstein was aware that Ashley's tumour was firm, without its own supply of blood vessels. This was as good a confirmation as any that the tumour was benign rather than cancerous. But the laboratory results would give the final verdict.

It was always difficult to know when to stop removing 'the enemy'. Instinctively the temptation was to continue until every bit was gone. That could be dangerous. Fred Epstein always said: 'If a brain-stem operation gets ruined, it happens in the last five minutes, when the neurosurgeon removes too much of the tumour.'

Fred Epstein had now debulked about 75 per cent of Ashley's tumour, perhaps more. He had taken out the root of the tumour. Now he hoped its branches and leaves would shrivel up and die. Ashley had been a very sick boy when he arrived at Fred's office yesterday. His disabilities were at an advanced stage. If Fred went any further, there might be permanent damage or Ashley might have a cardiac arrest in the operating theatre.

Even if he stopped now, there was always the real chance that something might have gone wrong. Fred recalled operating on Marco, a fourteen-year-old boy from northern Italy who was a skiing enthusiast. Everything went well and Marco was soon back on the slopes.

Three years later, Marco needed a second operation. This time he woke from the operation a paraplegic. Devastated, Fred recalled his own mother's comments on his poor grades at school: 'Did you try your best, Fred? Did you try your best?'

Fred Epstein paused and looked at his work on Ashley. He knew he had done his best. As a medical student he had switched to neurosurgery because of the excitement, risk and glamour of being at the top of the medical pantheon. 'I like to be on top, and I'm propelled by a need to be there,' he wrote in his book *Gifts of Time*. 'Maybe that's why I put PED-NS1—paediatric neurosurgeon one—on the licence plate of my Ferrari.'

His medical team waited expectantly for Fred's decision. They knew they couldn't influence him on how far to go with a tumour removal. Each was an expert at this kind of operation, but it was entirely Fred's decision.

Dr Fred Epstein put down his tools and stood back.

'OK. I think I've done all I can here,' he said, stretching his aching muscles. 'Now we've just got to wait and see what's going to happen.'

13 This Little Piggy

After Andrew left the operating theatre, he took off the gown and face mask and removed the disposable slippers. Then he, Vivien and Sue Roberton went out for a long walk. Andrew badly needed a haircut. The Press later said he had a haircut to calm his nerves. The fact was that his hair really *was* long and untidy. While Andrew was having his hair cut, Sue had her nails done by a manicurist. Vivien just sat and waited.

After that, they all went to their favourite eating place, the Gemini Diner, for a late breakfast. They tried to eat but were too churned up inside and left nearly full plates. They made a visit to the bank to get some much-needed cash. It was all a way of killing time until news of the operation came through.

Back at the hospital they visited the canteen and then sat in an area outside the ward that was a kind of conservatory. When the winter sun shone, it was pleasantly warm in there.

Vivien had none of the doubts that Andrew had entertained in the operating theatre. She instinctively knew that everything would be all right. God had told them to come to New York and she was sure Ashley would be OK. She also had a lot of confidence in Dr Epstein. As the hours dragged by, hope rose in Andrew, too. If something had gone wrong, surely they would have been told about it straight away—wouldn't they?

While they waited they met an Israeli couple whose son, David, had previously been operated on by a doctor at the medical centre. The family had returned to New York because David's tumour had started to grow again. This time a surgeon other than Dr Epstein was operating on him. David's tumour, Andrew and Vivien discovered, was in a different position from Ashley's, so maybe Ashley's wouldn't grow back like David's had.

At last, after they had waited hours and hours, Fred Epstein appeared.

'Andrew and Vivien, I've just come out of the operating theatre.'

'Yes, yes,' Vivien said, excitement mounting in her.

'Well, it's good news. The operation's been a success so far, and I couldn't be more pleased with the outcome. We've managed to get something like 75 to 90 per cent of the tumour out. The worst part of the operation's over. But it's still going to take between one and a half and two hours to close up Ashley's wound.'

'Thank you,' said Vivien, rushing up to hug and kiss Fred. 'You're an angel, and I'm so happy!'

A short while later Fred Epstein told the BBC television crew: 'Ashley's mother gave me a big hug and a kiss and made my day!'

It wasn't Fred's first TV interview that afternoon. Unknown to Ashley's parents, the TV camera team that had been in the operating theatre had spoken to him as soon as he had finished his part of the operation, while he was still in his gown. The interview, together with film of part of the operation, had already been beamed by satellite to evening news viewers in the UK.

Sue Roberton went back to the hotel to phone England and break the exciting news to family and friends. Although only twenty minutes had elapsed since Fred Epstein had spoken to Andrew and Vivien, people in the UK already knew the operation had been a success.

When they heard what had happened, Andrew and Vivien, as the parents, were disappointed that the media had broken news of their son's operation to millions of people before they even knew about it. Surely they could have waited until Andrew and Vivien had told their relatives before releasing the news?

Meanwhile, back in the operating theatre, the section of Ashley's backbone was replaced and attached with stitches through the other bones. The dura was stitched back with silk sutures and the muscles and skin closed up. A sterile dressing was applied and Ashley was nearly ready to return to the recovery room.

First, though, there was the all-important check for any neurological damage. If Ashley's spinal cord or brain stem had been injured in any way during the operation, he could be permanently paralyzed from the neck downwards.

After disconnecting the gas supply, Murray Canter, the anaesthetist, bent over Ashley, working hard to bring him around. Carefully, he checked Ashley's pupils and tested his reflexes. Then came the critical point.

'OK, Ashley, let's play that game. Remember it? "This little piggy." Wiggle your toes, all of them.'

There was a delay, as if Ashley hadn't heard him. Murray's heart skipped a beat. What if something had gone horribly wrong at this late stage?

'Come on, Ashley, wiggle your toes.'

As he watched, first one then the rest of Ashley's toes began to wiggle.

'Good boy!' he said enthusiastically, breathing a sigh of relief. 'Tell Fred he can let the boy's parents visit him in the recovery room,' he said to a fellow doctor.

Ashley's operation had lasted a total of seven hours and forty minutes. Now it was all over.

Seeing Ashley in the recovery room was a very frightening experience for both Andrew and Vivien. Ashley was connected to a series of monitors and was still on a ventilator. Normally the anaesthetist would have removed the breathing tube and other leads and wires, leaving just the intravenous line, to supply fluids and prevent dehydration, and a drainage tube from the wound. But Ashley's tumour had been in the region of the brain stem, where breathing is controlled, so it was vital that he was helped with his breathing—just in case.

As Andrew and Vivien walked into the room, Ashley was trying his best to push the tube out of his mouth. He was also trying to cry, but no sound came out because of the tube. Was he struggling to breathe? Had he survived this huge operation to die right now? No, surely not.

A nurse rushed over and ushered them out of the room. They put Ashley back under anaesthetic and resited the tube in the correct position. Once this was completed, Andrew and Vivien were let back in to see their son. They bent over Ashley, struck by how peaceful he looked after such a long ordeal.

'I love you, Ashley,' whispered Vivien, tears welling up in her eyes. 'The nasty thing in your head's gone. Dr Epstein managed to get rid of it for you. Isn't that good?'

She could see that, even though Ashley was still drowsy from the anaesthetic, he was relieved.

Although Fred Epstein was exhausted from the surgery, his day had only just begun. The Press hounded him, asking for more and more interviews. It seemed as if the whole world wanted to know the exciting news that Ashley's operation had been a success.

'From a technical point of view, the surgery went better than I expected, considering how fragile and ill Ashley was,' Dr Epstein explained to the waiting Press. 'I was able to remove 70 to 95 per cent of the tumour and I'm hopeful it won't grow back again. We'll be watching him very carefully for a few days, especially his breathing, watching for infection and to see that the wound heals.'

He explained to the Press that he had carried out 500 operations similar to Ashley's. A brain-stem tumour was very rare in Britain, with only two or three cases a year. He dealt with thirty or forty cases a year from all over the world. 'There's no need for Ashley to come back to us for further treatment,' he said boldly. 'I wouldn't have done the operation if I didn't think it would have worked.'

Ashley was making a more rapid recovery than anyone could have imagined. Within hours of coming out of the operating theatre he had to be sedated after he tried to remove all his tubes and wires. The doctors didn't think he was ready to breathe on his own—but Ashley did.

Fred Epstein told Andrew and Vivien that there was a 99.99 per cent chance that the tissue he had removed was benign. What was left would probably just shrivel up. He added that if Ashley had not been so weakened by the steroids and radiotherapy treatment he had been given in England, Fred might well have been able to remove

137

even more of the tumour. He told them it would have been too dangerous even to attempt to remove any more.

Back in Kent the *Gravesend Reporter* had a headline on 3 November 1994: 'Pray for Ashley's recovery.' The Fowle family's long-term babysitter, Lee Rawlinson, was reported as saying that Gravesend Christian Fellowship had been praying hard for some good news. 'Prayer and fasting sessions have been held every Tuesday for weeks,' he said. 'We knew God would hear our prayers.'

Cards began flooding in to the family home in Northfleet, Kent, ready for Ashley's homecoming. Some were sent on to New York while many others were kept ready for their return. Simon's whole class signed a special, homemade card for Ashley.

Simon and Michelle, together with Aunt Angie, produced a scrap album during the time away. It began: 'Once upon a time there was a happy family... until they found out in February 1994 that Ashley had a brain-stem tumour.'

The scrapbook, which contained cards, Press cuttings and drawings, told how radiotherapy failed to help him. 'Very soon Ashley's breathing wasn't good. He was tiring easily. It was difficult for him to move. His limbs were becoming immobile.

'Slowly, the hours and days, weeks and months, were ticking away. We all watched as our little boy deteriorated.'

The book finished on a high note as the surgery was successful and Ashley's condition in New York began to improve.

One of Andrew's colleagues, Peter Harman, visited Simon and Michelle regularly while their parents and Ashley were away. He was a big, cuddly policeman with a lively sense of humour. One day he and some of Andrew's other colleagues showed Simon, Michelle and their Aunt Angie around Maidstone police station. Simon and Michelle were locked in the prison cells, much to their delight.

The Press continued to be interested in Ashley's operation. Following the intensive publicity for the New York University Medical Centre, a group of paediatric neurosurgeons decided to send out a leaflet explaining that there were also experts in childhood neurosurgery and with the necessary equipment in England. William Harkness and Richard Hayward, both paediatric neurosurgeons at Great Ormond Street Hospital for Sick Children, blamed themselves for the lack of publicity.

Richard Hayward said: 'Paediatric neurosurgeons never get much recognition and there has always been a reticence about self-publicity. Added to that, we are up against a very good publicity machine at the New York centre.

'We have the equipment here, we have the expertise, and we have the continuing care. The children going to New York may come back a week after the operation. If anything goes wrong, it is the NHS that looks after them.'

Later, they commented on children such as Ashley Fowle and Alicia McCluckie receiving treatment in the US.

'These operations should have been carried out in this country,' said Richard Hayward, senior paediatric neurosurgeon at Great Ormond Street Hospital. 'We've met the Department of Health and we want to see a guideline on referrals as soon as possible.'

Richard Hayward continued: 'Clearly, patients like these will not be treated properly unless they are concentrated in a few specialist units. I think what happens is that a child is treated in a centre where there isn't a neurosurgeon involved in the care of children, and they therefore will not get into a system where treatment of their type of problem is an everyday event.'

Mrs McCluckie, mother of three-year-old Alicia, was told in New York that the equipment was available in the UK but that it was 'primitive'. A spokesman for the National Health Service said: 'Our technology is not in a primitive state.'

Dr Fred Epstein told the Press: 'The bulk of the patients could have been treated in the UK. It seems as though it is easier to come here to get a second opinion than to go 100 miles in the UK. What I've perceived is that in the UK there is a certain lack of inter-constitutional collaboration.'

Dr Epstein observed that the National Health Service had not moved with the times. 'My perception is that your system is a much more traditional one, a pyramid system with the professor at the top and where one pyramid doesn't talk to another. I think it needs adjusting. Patients like these should be referred to specialists who can make the appropriate decisions.'

At the hospital in New York the pathology report on the tumour indicated that there was no trace of the cancerous *ependymoma* suggested by the British pathologist. It was thought that the British doctor might not have removed enough tissue to make an accurate diagnosis. Ashley's tumour was rediagnosed as an *'astrocytoma, diffuse fibrillary type grade I/III'*—a much less serious one.

Ashley had the breathing tube removed twenty-four hours after his operation. It was much earlier than the doctors had expected.

Soon afterwards, Ashley looked up at Andrew, speaking for the first time in a day and a half.

'I want to go home, Daddy,' he said.

Ashley had an MRI scan four days after the surgery. It gave rise to even better news than Dr Epstein had at first thought. There was hardly any tumour left, just a large empty space. By Sunday, five days after surgery, all Ashley's wires and tubes were removed and he was ready to be moved from the intensive care unit back into the drab surroundings of Nine West. It was a plain ward, with few decorations. New York's East River could be glimpsed from the windows of some of the wards, but not this one.

The move was a cause for celebration. It also happened on Andrew's birthday, which was another reason to celebrate. Ashley gave his dad a tie covered in dollar symbols while Vivien gave him a couple of New York sweatshirts.

It was also a sad day, because Sue Roberton, the Police Welfare officer, was due to fly back to England the next morning. The three adults had done almost everything together during the past week. Sue had become almost a part of the family.

Unfortunately, Ronald McDonald House hadn't felt the same way. After Sue had spent two nights there, she was asked to leave because she wasn't a relative. She then had to find somewhere else to stay. It was the week of the New York Marathon, and most hotels in the city were full. The only one she could find had a plush reception area but the rooms were dreadful. Hers was tiny and cramped, with mould on the walls and peeling wallpaper. It smelled musty and stale. For the 'privilege' of staying there she paid the princely sum of $200 a night. At least she had freshly laundered towels each day.

During the week, she had been tempted to stay in New York for good. Fred Epstein could see her many good qualities and offered her a job as his welfare officer. Although she appreciated his offer, she had to turn it down.

By now, Andrew was suffering from severe neck aches, brought on by the stress of the last few weeks. He had a massage at a health salon in New York, far away from the seedier side of massage in New York's red light district.

Life on Nine West began to get back to normal for Ashley. Among regular visitors were a group of clowns from the Big Apple Circus. They were volunteers who went to hospitals throughout New York bringing cheer to children of all ages. One clown visited Ashley soon after he came out of intensive care. He stuck a red nose on Ashley, tussled up his hair and made him laugh for the camera.

Another clown, with ginger hair, took a great liking to Andrew's English accent. Every time Andrew spoke, the clown burst into delighted laughter. When he found that Andrew was a policeman as well, it really made his day. From then on, the clown went around with his thumbs in his lapels and his knees bent, in the caricature of the English bobby, saying: 'Evenin' all,' and: "Ello, 'ello, 'ello. What 'ave we 'ere?'

Fred Epstein and his team of medical staff were among the most caring professionals Andrew and Vivien had ever come across. They each had their unique characteristics.

Fred himself was a busy man who never seemed to have time to eat. His office ended up littered with half-eaten takeaways. Sometimes he would take a cracker or biscuit off a passing tray and would talk to Vivien or Andrew while eating it, the crumbs dropping down his suit and onto the floor.

Fred's two partners, Jeff Wisoff and Rick Abbott, were also involved in Ashley's care. Jeff Wisoff was described by Fred Epstein as 'my brilliant associate'. He was thin-faced with glasses and a small moustache. He was a pioneer when it came to operations. Rick was dark-haired with boyish looks. He, too, was a pioneer neurosurgeon.

Another doctor on Fred's team, George Gello, was a handsome Italian-American with short dark hair, Mediterranean looks and a delightful smile. He was a pleasant man in the same league as Richard Gere. George often brought Ashley chocolates to eat. Vivien took an instant liking to him. 'My mother fancies you,' Ashley said to him once, with a cheeky grin.

Another member of Epstein's team, the paediatric neuro-oncologist Jeff Allen, looked and sounded like Big Bird from Sesame Street. He even carried a flashlight with a picture of Big Bird on it. Once, when Jeff came to check the young English patient, to Vivien's embarrassment Ashley blurted out: 'Mummy thinks you're Big Bird!'

Tania Shiminski-Maher was Fred Epstein's nurse-practitioner. She was a pleasant-looking young woman with glasses who had a great skill at helping families in crisis. She could explain to them what was happening and help them through the time of rehabilitation and adjusting to an illness that might recur.

Lynn O'Dell was the hospital's Press Officer. She had to cope with the numerous questions about Ashley from the Press. 'This Ashley,' she said after dealing with hundreds of faxes and phone calls. 'I'll be glad when he goes home so I can have a rest!'

Finally, there were the administrators, JoAnn Baldwin and her two assistants, Rochelle Sedita and Natalie Cutrone. Rochelle was in charge of scheduling.

The next few days went quickly. Ashley made great improvements every day and on Friday 11 November 1994, ten days after his operation, he was discharged from the New York University Medical Centre with instructions to get on with life as quickly as possible. His only medications apart from the steroids were a couple of antibiotics, paracetemol (acetaminophen) as a painkiller and an iron supplement.

At the end of Ashley's stay, Andrew and Vivien bought a copy of Fred Epstein's book, *Gifts of Time,* written with Elaine Fantle Shinberg (1993, William Morrow & Company Inc, New York). Fred wrote in it: 'For Ashley, my favourite patient. Next time visit New York as a tourist. Thank you for making us both look good! Love, Fred Epstein.'

The prognosis Fred Epstein now gave Andrew and Vivien was that the tumour had been benign and that Ashley had a 90 per cent chance of living a long life with no regrowth of tumour.

Without the operation, Ashley would have been dead within six months to a year.

14 Strong as Superman

After so many days apart, Andrew, Vivien and Ashley were together again, staying in the room at Ronald McDonald House. It was about three-quarters of an hour's walk from the medical centre, situated on East 73rd Street between First and York Avenues, close to the Queensborough Bridge.

The house was the largest Ronald McDonald House in the world, holding 300 to 400 people. It had a big glass front with double doors. In a city of automation, it was surprising that the doors weren't automatic. This made it difficult to get a child in a pushchair or wheelchair in and out.

Inside, there was a tall reception hall with a high ceiling that went up to the second floor. There was a glass partition around that floor and it was possible to see people walking around on the landing. There was a reception desk on the right, with the administration offices behind.

In the middle of the reception hall was a seating area that went around a brick-built planter containing tall indoor plants. There were two elevators straight ahead of them.

Andrew and Vivien's bedroom was about 25ft long with en suite bath, shower and toilet. There were two single beds plus a camp bed for Ashley. The TV could receive seventy-four channels—a big difference from the four channels they could normally get in England. There was a desk, a chest of drawers and a huge, walk-in wardrobe. It was pleasantly decorated and was more like a four- or five-star hotel than a 'home from home'.

Each family was allocated a small kitchen on arrival that they had to share with one or more other families. They were expected to prepare food there and eat it in the communal dining room. Eating and drinking in the bedrooms was strictly forbidden.

Sometimes, despite the rule, Vivien would sneak cups of coffee or a takeaway pizza into the bedroom. She was never caught.

Andrew and Vivien were allocated the smallest of the kitchens. They had to share it with a very impolite South American family. The woman in particular was extremely arrogant to the point of rudeness and would literally push Vivien out of the way if she wanted to get to the dishwasher or cooker. Eventually, Andrew and Vivien could bear the situation no longer and avoided the kitchen as much as they could.

Although the food wasn't included in the price of their stay, sometimes Ronald McDonald House would lay on a special meal for the families. It wasn't always Big Macs and milk shakes, either. Once they had a huge spread of all kinds of Italian food. Another time there was a massive breakfast with as much as they could eat.

One evening the Body Shop came to the house and organized a kind of Generation Game. A woman demonstrated how to fill a basket with Body Shop products, then shrinkwrap it. Everyone was then given a little basket and had to fill it with soaps, cosmetics and body lotions for women. Once that was done, the demonstrator shrinkwrapped each one and gave it to the person who filled it. Even Andrew made a pretty basket, though he didn't have much use for the contents.

The Ronald McDonald House had a big library and a huge playroom in the basement full of toys and games.

Like all other New York residents, Andrew and Vivien had to sort out their garbage into separate bags for glass, paper, plastic and metal. Then they put each bag down the correct chute. Vivien made a mistake once and put the wrong bag down the wrong chute. She wondered if she would be visited by one of the special garbage patrol police, whose job was to enforce the strict recycling laws.

There were aluminium can recycling machines in many of the stores and these dispensed five cents for every can put in. Andrew was interested to see the homeless people each morning sorting through the waste bins collecting huge sacks of hundreds of cans to put in the machine and earn their money for the day.

Most of the people in the Ronald McDonald House were friendly and understanding. Andrew and Vivien got on especially well with the Gould family, who stayed in the room opposite to them. Andrew had met Roger Gould and his son Jo by accident on the day of Ashley's operation. He was going through the double doors and held them open for a man pushing a boy in a wheelchair. When Andrew spoke to the man he replied: 'Oh, you're from England, are you?'

'Yeah, that's right.'

'I'm Roger Gould, and this is my son, Jo.'

'Hi. I'm Andrew Fowle. My son Ashley just had his operation today.'

'Where's that?'

'At the New York University Medical Centre. Dr Epstein's the surgeon.'

'Oh, yes. Jo was there under Fred Epstein. Now he's been referred to Dr Finlay at the Sloan Kettering Hospital. We heard there was another English couple coming.'

They kept meeting each other and soon Andrew and Vivien became friendly with the whole family—Roger and Michelle, their daughter Hollie and their very sick ten-year-old son, Jo.

Each day, Ashley spent time with the physiotherapist at the hospital. Christy Worsoe had helped Ashley soon after he was out of intensive care by 'kick-starting' him back into action. She taught him how to use his left arm, his right arm now being almost immobile. She helped him relearn basic movements—getting up on his hands and knees, sitting up without losing his balance and rolling over in one movement. Sometimes Ashley would be sweating with the effort but it was worth it in the end. Christy gave him a lot of her spare time free of charge and visited them at Ronald McDonald House.

They decided to go to church the following Sunday.

Just before they had gone to the US, Andrew had asked his church leader, Dave Webster, if he knew of any good churches in New York.

'No, but there must be lots. I'll make some enquiries and let you know.'

After they had been in New York for a couple of weeks, Dave rang to tell Andrew about a book he had been reading, *Catch the Fire,* by Guy Chevreau. At the back of the book there was a section on the effect that the Holy Spirit was having on churches in the US. One of those churches happened to be Manhattan/New York City Vineyard Church. The piece had been written by its pastor, Mike Turrigiano.

'You won't believe this,' he said. 'I've just finished this book and there's something about a good church in Manhattan. Why don't you call in and see them?'

'Do you have the address?'

'No, but you can look it up in a phone book.'

They phoned reception and asked if anyone knew how to get to the church. Five minutes later the phone in their room rang and a man at the other end introduced himself as Lyall, one of the church leaders. The receptionist had apparently rung the church office for them. Lyall gave directions for getting to the meeting and finished with: 'See you on Sunday.'

Now they set off, Ashley in his pushchair. At the door of the house they met the security guard.

'Mornin',' he said pleasantly.

'Good morning.'

'Where are you off to today?'

'We're going to church.'

'What church is that?''

'It's Vineyard Manhattan Church.'

'Where's that?'

They told him the address, which was in Harlem on 103rd Street West and Amsterdam Avenue.

'103rd Street? That's one of the worst areas in Manhattan. Did you know that anything higher than 96th Street is in the dangerous area?'

'No.'

'Er—how are you going to get there?'

'Walk. Why?'

'Well, I wouldn't advise you to walk. I'll call a cab for you.'

'What's the problem?'

'It's a real well known bad part of town. You could get mugged, or even knifed or shot. When you get there, before you get out of the cab make sure you check all around. It's not a very nice neighbourhood. Oh, yes, and make sure you know what sort of place you're going to. There are some real weird churches in that neighbourhood.'

They thanked him for his advice and were soon in a bright yellow New York cab heading for one of New York's roughest areas.

When they arrived after their $11 ride, they took the security guard's advice and looked around carefully. The cab had stopped outside a residential youth centre a bit like a YMCA. The streets were empty of people and they noticed that most of the buildings were decorated with brightly coloured graffiti.

Fearfully, they emerged from the taxi. *If God's brought us here, he's not going to lead us into danger*, thought Andrew. *We need to believe he's here with us.*

Once in the building they had to state their business to a man behind a desk and then sign in. They took the elevator to the second floor, walked down a corridor and turned left into another corridor. They came across another desk in the corridor, covered in leaflets about the church. There they were met by a friendly young woman with a big smile. Serena Page-Bailey was English but now living in New York. She was delighted that they, too, were from England and they spent a few minutes chatting together.

Seeing Ashley in his pushchair, she ushered them into a room that served as the creche. Here they were introduced to some of the church people. There was Lauri Mah, a pretty girl with long, dark hair and classic

Chinese features. She fell in love with Ashley, treating him like her son.

By contrast there was Nathan Bowie, a gentle giant of a man with the looks and build of boxing champion Frank Bruno.

Equally big was Eric Kech, a huge white man who played quarterback in American football, and his slim, petite wife Beth. Eric was a bit like a scruffier version of Arnold Schwarzenegger.

They spent a long time talking with everyone in the creche. Only when they felt Ashley was happy could they leave him there and make their way into the main church. He was happily playing with Zion, Eric and Beth's three-year-old daughter.

The building they were in was a modern one typical of New York. This part of the building was designed to look like an old English chapel. It had a high arched ceiling with a huge window. The only difference between this church in New York and a typical parish church in rural England was that there were individual plastic chairs and carpet instead of wooden pews and a cold stone floor.

The room was rented each Sunday from another church that also used it. It was big enough to hold 200 people, though there were only about fifty or sixty on the day Andrew and Vivien arrived. They were struck by the fact that most of the people were young, and there was a lively worship band to lead the singing.

The church's leader was Mike Turrigiano. He was an Italian-American with short, greying black hair, a little beard and round, metal-framed glasses. Mike was very caring for the church people. He was also interested in helping needy and deprived people, particularly those who lived in Harlem and the Bronx, another notorious area of New York.

They enjoyed their visit and decided to go back the following week. After their second visit, the Fowles joined Eric and Beth for brunch. Eric ate like a horse. While Andrew and Vivien had a couple of delicious homemade waffles each, Eric had a plate piled high with them. They felt as if they belonged in this city and this family.

That afternoon, Eric took them on a sightseeing tour of Manhattan in his big spacewagon. They went through China Town and Greenwich Village—the gay section— and then stopped for a stodgy, sickly-sweet ice cream in Little Italy. Even Ashley, with his liking for sweet things, found it too rich.

Another man they met at the church was Paul Strait, a student doctor who used to be a highly paid lawyer. He was the kind of person who went for a qualification, worked for a time in the profession and then moved on. Like Eric, Paul later showed Andrew and Vivien the sights of New York.

The Paediatric Neuro-Oncology Tumour Board met on 16 November 1994 and discussed Ashley's case. Among the board's members were some of the US's top neuro-surgeons specializing in children, including Fred Epstein. Their recommendations included close clinical follow-up to check the long-term effects of radiation—thyroid problems, heart difficulties and secondary tumours. They wanted Ashley's steroids gradually phased out and regular MRI scans for the first year. They also said it was essential that physiotherapy be continued to avoid further problems with Ashley's movements.

On Thanksgiving Day, 23 November 1994, church leader Mike Turrigiano invited a number of people from the church to his home for dinner, including Andrew, Vivien and Ashley.

First there was a huge mountain of pasta and sausages. Andrew and Vivien were convinced that was the main course, but it was only the starter. Soon there was turkey with all the accompaniments, including cranberry sauce, followed by pumpkin pie.

Andrew and Vivien were treated like a long-lost brother and sister. They were welcomed with open arms and they felt as if they had come home.

Everyone was delighted to meet Ashley. Char Turrigiano, Mike's wife, gave him a huge soft puppet called Sophie that was even bigger than he was.

While they were fitting into New York life, the Fowles continued to keep in touch with people in England. Ashley spoke to Lee Rawlinson three weeks after his operation. Lee told the Press afterwards: 'Ashley told me he was as strong as Superman and the Gladiators, his favourite TV stars.'

Vivien's parents came over to New York and they all went on a boat trip out to the Statue of Liberty. There were so many people waiting to go up the famous monument that they gave up and got back in the boat again. But it was a lovely trip nevertheless.

One day the *Daily Mirror* phoned them up.

'We've been asked by Walt Disney World to find a special child to switch on the Christmas tree lights there,' the journalist said. 'We'd like Ashley to do it.'

They put the idea to Fred Epstein, who couldn't see any problems with it. They told the *Daily Mirror,* who agreed to fly the three of them, as well as Simon and Michelle, to Walt Disney World. They would travel to Orlando, Florida, on Tuesday 6 December, have a family reunion and spend a week there before flying home together.

One day at their home in Kent, Simon and Michelle were presented with a huge homemade card with a colourful picture of Mickey Mouse as the Sorcerer's Apprentice. 'Guess what, Simon and Michelle?' the card said. 'Hey kids, what say you about a trip to Disney?'

The card was signed by family friends and members of the Police Benevolent Fund.

'Nobody deserves this more than you two for all the times you've been so understanding and well-behaved throughout these difficult times,' wrote Angie Fowle, Andrew's sister, who was staying with the children while their parents and brother were away. 'One day, when you're all grown up, you'll be able to look back at this as a new beginning for Ashley and for you two with Mummy and Daddy. Have a lovely holiday.'

Everything was set for the trip. Then, suddenly, on Sunday 4 December, two days before they were due to fly to Florida, Ashley developed a high temperature that seemed to be getting worse and worse. They phoned Fred Epstein at home.

'Take him to the emergency room at the hospital straight away,' he told them as soon as he heard the symptoms. There was a sense of urgency in his voice.

Panic seized Vivien. Her unspoken fear was being realized. After all the progress Ashley had made since his operation, could an infection have crossed through the wound into his skull? Could his soaring temperature mean he was now suffering from meningitis?

15 Snow White Delight

Andrew and Vivien rushed Ashley straight to the emergency room at the New York University Medical Centre. By then his temperature had reached 104 degrees Fahrenheit. The doctors gave him an injection that helped to reduce the temperature. Then they decided to re-admit him.

Andrew had noticed that in the nape of Ashley's neck he had a scab. Since the operation he had been wearing a neck collar and the Velcro used to fix it around his neck had knocked the scab off. The area had become red and wouldn't heal up. By now it appeared more yellow than red. Andrew and Vivien had put dressings on it but it just didn't seem to heal. The skin either side was pulled in as if it were being held by a stitch.

'I think they left a stitch in,' Andrew commented to a doctor.

The doctor used some scissors to try to cut the stitch. The scissors went further and further into the hole until they had almost disappeared! Then, as the doctor started pulling the scissors out, a big pool of yellow pus gushed out with them.

'There's no stitch in there,' he said. 'Ashley's got a bad infection.'

The nurses cleaned it all out, leaving a massive hole under the skin in Ashley's neck. They plugged the hole with special wadding soaked in antibiotic and put him on an intravenous antibiotic. Their concern, like Vivien's, was that the infection would get into Ashley's brain and he would end up with meningitis.

Ashley had a CT scan to check whether any infection had crossed through into the brain. Once it was ready, the doctor held up the scan. 'There's no sign of infection inside there. But this is where the tumour was,' he said, pointing to an empty space on the film.

Vivien's heart leapt for joy as realization struck her. Although Ashley was suffering from an infection of his wound, the tumour that had nearly destroyed his life looked as if it had gone.

The next day Andrew and Vivien spoke to Dr Epstein.

'We're due to fly to Florida tomorrow,' Andrew told him. 'Do you think Ashley will be all right to go?'

'Yeah, no worries. Whatever happens, I'll make sure you get there.'

He even offered to arrange for a doctor he knew in Florida to look after Ashley so they could still make the journey.

Andrew stayed with Ashley in the hospital overnight on Monday. The following morning, the day they were due to travel, Andrew woke to find Ashley's pillow saturated in yellow pus. He sat Ashley up and found that another hole had appeared higher up along the line of the operation. A steady stream of pus was coming out of this hole as well as the first one.

Andrew called the nurse.

'I don't think we'll be flying to Florida today,' he said gloomily.

She took one look. 'No, I don't think so, either.'

When Fred Epstein saw the wound he advised Andrew and Vivien to call in the services of a plastic surgeon. Plastic surgery is considered to be the same as cosmetic surgery. Once, a small child under Fred Epstein's care had had an abscess in the space left by a tumour. The abscess damaged a section of bone, which had to be removed. The opening was repaired by a plastic surgeon, and the health insurance company refused to pay up.

'A plastic surgeon is utilized in this type of operation because it is very difficult to close a wound of this kind,' he wrote to them. 'An area that has previously been operated on needs a very tight closure so that you will not have leakage of cerebrospinal fluid.' What he didn't mention to the insurance company was that small children are also concerned about their appearance, but that's very important to Fred, too.

The plastic surgeon they called in was Dr Zaid. Although he was brilliant at his job, his attitude was totally the opposite to that of Fred Epstein and his team. He had few bedside manners and seemed totally uninterested in his young patients.

He looked at Ashley and said: 'OK, we'll open the wound up and clean it all out.' Then he went away. Ashley was given fresh dressing changes to absorb the pus. He would be taken back into the operating room to have the wound opened in the hope that it would heal better.

By the time this became clear it was too late to call off the trip to Walt Disney World. Simon and Michelle, together with their grandmother and Aunt Angie, were already on the plane. They were planning to have a big family reunion at the hotel in Florida. Andrew and Vivien phoned Orlando and left a message for them: 'Sorry, we can't come. Ashley is back in hospital to have another operation. We love you. Mummy and Daddy.'

Simon and Michelle were upset that they couldn't be with their parents and Ashley, but they still managed to have the time of their lives.

When Vivien realized they couldn't go to Florida, she was desperately upset. She had set her hopes on it and now those hopes had been dashed. After such a long time apart from Simon and Michelle, she felt really disappointed. It had been like a dream come true having a reunion in Walt Disney World.

The delay made Vivien realize how much she was pining for her other children. She couldn't stop crying. As a mother she was thinking: *It's a couple of weeks before Christmas and we haven't got anything in—no presents or food. How can I give my children a happy Christmas?*

Fred Epstein saw their disappointed faces and Vivien's tears. He came up with an idea.

'Look, I know how upset you are that you can't meet up with your other two children. What I'll do is this. At my expense I'll fly them from Florida to New York, put them up in a top hotel and give you a blank cheque. It doesn't matter what their expenses are here. Don't worry, I'll pay them.'

Whatever Fred Epstein's motives in being a world famous surgeon, money certainly didn't seem to be one of them! It was a generous offer, and Andrew and Vivien found it very tempting. But they weren't sure how long Ashley was going to be in hospital. In addition, Simon and Michelle would have to come to New York, then go home to England again. There would be a reunion, but only a temporary one.

Staying in Walt Disney World for a week, they would have a fantastic time and then fly home. At least when their parents and Ashley flew from New York to England, it was going to be for good, and there would be no more painful separation. After thinking it through, this was their decision.

'Thanks for your very generous offer, Dr Epstein,' Andrew said. 'But we think it may not be the best thing.'

It was now touch and go whether they would be back in time for Christmas. At one point the doctors were talking about Ashley being in hospital over Christmas and right up to April. 'Usually the wound stays open for three months or more,' someone said to them.

On 7 December Andrew told the *Daily Mail:* 'We're hoping to be back in time for Christmas. Our main concern is making sure that Ashley is OK.'

In the operating theatre, Dr Zaid reopened the wound, scraped out the infection and cleaned the wound, then left it open. Dr George Gello, the dark-haired Italian American on Epstein's team, was involved in Ashley's care after the minor operation. He put antibiotic in the wound and made sure that three times a day Ashley had fresh changes of dressing soaked in antibiotic. Gradually, over several days, the wound closed itself. Dr Zaid had left in some 'bootlace' stitches. Towards the end, after the wound had closed up, Ashley was taken back into the operating theatre. Dr Zaid pulled the stitches tight and the wound was closed like the laces of a boot. The wound had a drain in it for two days and it was then removed.

Dr Zaid was a clever plastic surgeon who also worked for the police and was interested that Andrew was a policeman. But his attitude was not friendly. He would visit Ashley for a few moments, then go away and not show up again for several days.

By now Ashley was beginning to complain about hospital food. Although his food was included in the price of the hospital stay, it never varied. He was given chicken virtually every day. His parents thought he would soon grow feathers and wings if he had any more. Sometimes, they brought in McDonald's hamburgers for Ashley just to give him some variety.

While Ashley was in hospital with his infection, Eric and Beth Kech babysat at the hospital on Andrew and Vivien's wedding anniversary, 11 December, so they could go out together. They went up the Empire State Building and walked around the balcony in the freezing cold.

While Ashley was being treated for his infection, Andrew and Vivien got to know another mother, Suzie, whose daughter had an eating disorder. Every parent had a different way of coping. Suzie coped by being obsessed with cleanliness. She brought in a bottle of bleach and went around disinfecting every surface in the ward. She also spent much of her time complaining about the mess everywhere.

When Suzie's daughter was discharged, Vivien saw a different aspect to this mother. She didn't leave the room as she had expected to find it. Instead, she left in her trail so much mess that a rat would have complained. There was a disgusting trail of crumbs, garbage all over the floor, paper, yoghurt pots and a host of other things. Suzie, it seemed, was the ultimate Jekyll and Hyde character.

Once Ashley's wound had healed, he could leave hospital. But his parents were warned to take care of him. Because of the radiotherapy the skin cells in his neck would heal a lot more slowly than normal, which could lead to another infection.

On Wednesday 14 December Andrew, Vivien and Ashley went to John F. Kennedy Airport, New York, in a taxi that Ronald McDonald House had ordered for them. All the people they knew were either students or working so there was no one available to see them off. They caught an American Airlines plane for the two-and-a-half-hour flight to Orlando, Florida. The *Daily Mirror* had decided to finance the trip, despite the delay.

They left New York with mixed feelings. They were glad of the much-needed break in Florida. All the worry and stress was beginning to come to an end. Now they had hope for the future.

They were also sad at leaving behind the people they had come to love and appreciate at the church and the hospital. They loved New York and had met many caring people. Andrew even thought about applying to the New York Police Department for a transfer from Kent.

At Orlando they were welcomed by Tom, one of Walt Disney World's hospitality/public relations people. He was a pleasant man who really took to Ashley. He and his wife couldn't have children themselves, but they enjoyed giving other people's children a great time.

Andrew, Vivien and Ashley stayed at the Contemporary Resort in the Disney complex right outside the Magic Kingdom theme park. They arrived at the Contemporary at about five in the evening and were shown to their room.

The Contemporary was a fifteen-storey hotel complex with an A-frame tower. A monorail went right through the middle of it at fourth floor level. Looking from the balcony on their floor they could see the restaurants below with the monorail running above them.

They went to bed after a long walk exploring the hotel itself. It had a swimming pool, a health and fitness centre, a sauna and a massage parlour. It also had a hairdresser's shop, where Andrew had his hair cut—again!

That night they were woken at 11.30 to the sound of very loud music. Their room overlooked Bay Lake.

There in the lake was a dragon, all lit up with music blaring away. It was actually a tug boat pulling a load of small boats, decorated with lights to look like a dragon.

They got up the following morning and went to a Character Breakfast. All the Disney characters—Pluto, Mickey, Minnie, Donald—came to sit with them. Goofy sat at their table and started spoonfeeding Ashley. Snow White gave Ashley a big, sloppy kiss and left bright-red lipstick on Ashley's cheek. It made Andrew positively jealous!

Normally, Character Meals had to be booked well in advance. Because Ashley was considered a VIP they had passes for this one on their very first morning. The meals were already booked and paid for, but if they bought souvenirs or snacks they had to pay for them.

Walt Disney World, they discovered, was the world's single most popular tourist attraction. The whole site took up 1,100 sq km—roughly the same area as Manhattan Island which they had just left.

The trip had been kept as a surprise for Ashley, and he was delighted with it. Their tour guide was Debbie Marziale, who had also shown Princess Diana around. They were taken from place to place on the site in a chauffeur-driven Cadillac limousine. It was white with black leather seats. It was so comfortable and quiet Andrew reckoned it felt like driving on air.

Inevitably, they spent much of their time in the 100-acre Magic Kingdom park with its theme areas—Mainstreet US, Adventureland, Frontierland, Liberty Square, Fantasyland, Mickey's Starland and Tomorrowland, with its famous Space Mountain. In the park they enjoyed the freedom of many of the world's best-known rides. When they went on the rides they never had to line up. As VIPs they were taken straight to the front.

Andrew and Vivien had both always wanted to visit Walt Disney World but had never in their wildest dreams expected they would. They tried some of the rides, though they were careful what they let Ashley go on. Most memorable for Andrew was the Tower of Terror, which allowed passengers to free-fall for a couple of feet, then the walls would go up, giving the illusion of accelerating rapidly towards the ground.

Also at Walt Disney World was the 260-acre Epcot Centre with its World Showcase and theme areas representing countries on all five continents. Epcot also included the Future Earth, with its distinctive golf-ball shaped Spaceship Earth, and various space themes.

Disney-MGM Studios Park had displays centring around all the popular Disney cartoons and feature films. Ashley loved Mickey Avenue, where once again he could meet his favourite cartoon characters. They also saw, at least in passing, Blizzard Beach, Planet Hollywood, Typhoon Lagoon, River Country, Discovery Island and Pleasure Island.

During their visit they had various Press events. A Press photographer from the *Daily Mirror* as well as Disney's own photographer took pictures of Ashley with Mickey and Minnie. The same day, 15 December, Ashley was the special guest to switch on the lights of a 65ft (20m) Christmas tree. Surrounded by Disney singers, he threw pixie dust in the air and the tree magically lit up.

There was even snow to go with the Christmas theme. The 'snow' was really foam made by bubble machines on top of the buildings, which was then blown over the crowds by huge fans. The machines weren't left on for too long because the pavements would start to get slippery.

They had dinner one time in the Magic Kingdom castle. Ashley met Cinderella and got another big, sloppy kiss from her.

There were crowds of people watching the various photo-calls. Ashley, Andrew and Vivien were often the centre of attention. After the Press had left them alone, though, they could get on with enjoying the sights and sounds of Walt Disney World anonymously.

The most exciting thing for Andrew and Vivien was seeing Ashley's face when he met Mickey Mouse, Minnie and Donald Duck in the private enclosure set aside for

Press photographs. They watched as Ashley reached out and grabbed Mickey's nose, delight filling his face. He went on to meet Aladdin. He squealed with delight, laughing for all he was worth at the Hoop de Doo Wild West show, with its singers, dancers and cowboys. They had barbecue food—huge spare ribs, mountains of chicken and baked beans—while they watched.

They also went to a Christmas show and an outdoor candlelit carol service, followed by fireworks on one of the lakes. They had front-row seats. Even so late in the evening, it wasn't cold; it was more like an English summer evening. They walked around in teeshirts while their guide, more used to hot Florida summers, wore a thick winter coat.

On their last day they saw a car drive past with the veteran film star Mickey Rooney in it. He was on his way to put hand prints in some cement at the MGM studios.

They had a wonderful six days at Walt Disney World marred only by the sheer exhaustion they felt because of the stress of the previous few weeks. They also had the continuing worries about Ashley: 'What if his tumour grows? What if he starts to deteriorate?'

At the end of their visit, Andrew commented to the British Press: 'It's the perfect ending to one of the worst years of our lives.'

Before their flight home Andrew decided to take up Richard Branson's offer and phone him for some help. On their flight over they had travelled economy class, jammed in like sardines. Now, with his neck wound, Ashley couldn't sit up for long periods of time. In addition, the flight from Orlando to London was two hours longer than their trip over to New York.

He spoke to someone at Richard Branson's office. 'Is there any way you can help us make Ashley's flight a little more comfortable? He can't sit up for long periods because of the operation.'

'Don't worry,' the woman said. 'I'll have a word with Richard.' Richard Branson was on holiday in the Caribbean at the time.

A while later Andrew had a phone call from Gill Clements of the Police Benevolent Fund. 'The Fowles are now flying home first class!' she said. Richard Branson himself had given approval for them to upgrade their tickets.

First class was a very different world from economy class. They had reclining seats with TVs and very plush headphones. There were free drinks, including champagne, at the bar. The cabin staff came around giving out blankets.

'Would you like your footrest out, ma'am? Would you like a neck massage, sir?'

Nothing was too much for them to do. Andrew half expected one of them to say: 'Would you like me to peel a grape for you?'

The staff made up a little bed up for Ashley on the floor at the front of the plane. They warned that he might have to be put in a seat because of the turbulence that day.

'What would you like to drink?' asked one of the cabin staff.

'I'd love a cappuccino,' said Vivien.

'I'm afraid that's one thing we don't have,' she replied. 'But I've got a sachet in my bag that I've brought from home. I'd be happy for you to have mine.'

'No, don't worry,' said Vivien. 'I wouldn't take yours.'

In the end she made it and brought it to Vivien, much to Vivien's delight.

The turbulence was getting so bad that Vivien had to keep hold of her cup. The cappuccino tasted delicious but after two sips the plane hit a very big air pocket and Vivien spilled the whole cupful over her clothes. The stewardess rushed to her aid and offered to give her a brand new track suit, then get her clothes dry cleaned and sent on to her at Virgin Atlantic's expense. Vivien appreciated the offer but declined it. She didn't want to put them to any more trouble and couldn't imagine wearing a Virgin tracksuit home.

Later, the turbulence decreased and they were able to settle down.

As soon as they landed at Gatwick, the door of the plane opened and the three Fowles emerged before everyone else. Sue Roberton and Jan Berry were waiting to greet them at the entrance to the tunnel. Sue and Jan carried their bags and then they all travelled on a small motorized train provided by the airport. The trouble was, it was so slow, they felt like getting out and walking.

'Prepare yourself for a shock,' said Sue suddenly.

Andrew and Vivien looked aghast. They had managed to get this far with Ashley. Whatever could have gone wrong now?

16 'I'm a Star!'

The shock awaiting Andrew and Vivien was something they never imagined in their wildest dreams. As the little train carrying the three of them and their luggage arrived at the gate, they were confronted by a sea of Press people swarming to meet them. It was as if the Press were waiting for some famous pop star instead of their little son Ashley.

There were crowds of photographers, reporters and TV crews, all vying for the best position. Although things were organized in advance, the Press were fighting each other to get the best positions. One woman kept trying to take photographs but the man in front was constantly jumping up and getting in the way. Finally, in exasperation, she hit him sharply in the back and he moved over. After dozens of photographs were taken, they went into a room specially set aside for Press conferences. By the time everyone had gathered, it was mayhem in the room.

'That's when it all hit me that Ashley was better,' said Vivien later. 'The room was spinning and I just felt it was all so unreal.' She asked for a cup of coffee, but even that didn't revive her. As journalists spoke to her she kept seeing double and even triple. One face was bad enough, but two or three of the same face was overwhelming! The room continued to spin around.

As they began setting up their TV cameras and checking their tape recorders, one of the journalists asked Ashley what he wanted for Christmas.

Ashley, clutching his Teddy bear Gary Gatwick, a gift from Gatwick Airport, cast a critical eye around at the sea of Press reporters. 'I want a big bullet gun so I can shoot all you Press,' he said with a cheesy grin.

When they repeated the question on camera, he replied: 'I've already told you!' That brought a big laugh, especially from the newspaper reporters, who unlike radio and TV were able to quote Ashley's original comment.

Ashley often refused to co-operate with the Press. Whenever a tape recorder was switched on, he would refuse to speak, but as soon as it was off he would talk away. That brought many a journalist running back saying: 'Ashley, would you say that for the tape, please?' Each time he would reply cheekily: 'No!'

Towards the end of their journey to Gatwick they had nearly been diverted to Manchester at the last minute because of fog. *That would have put paid to all their plans,* thought Vivien, now recovering from the shock of so many journalists.

Andrew hadn't planned what to say in advance. It just all came out about the frustration he felt at the way their doctors in the UK virtually wrote Ashley off.

'We're pretty sick about the treatment Ashley got over here,' he told the crowd. 'We feel we've been lied to. You like to think your own doctors will do the best they can for your child, but they obviously haven't, and we're not happy at all. We've now met other parents who have gone through exactly what we have.'

Andrew was delighted with their visit to the US. 'We know we couldn't have received better treatment anywhere,' he said. 'The Americans were brilliant. They made all the difference to Ashley.'

While Ashley had been in the US, a group of British neurosurgeons specializing in children had hit back with a campaign to increase awareness of the facilities for brain and spinal tumours available under the National Health Service. They claimed that they could have done the surgery just as well as the New York University Medical Centre. For instance, two years previously eight-year-old Noel Ryan had been diagnosed with a brain tumour and had been successfully treated at Great Ormond Street Hospital within days.

Andrew commented on the campaign: 'We've been told since we've been in America that Great Ormond Street say they can do the operation. If that's the case, why weren't we told? We would have preferred to stay at home for the operation.'

On a brighter note, Andrew and Vivien were looking forward to a nice, quiet Christmas at home with the rest of the family. 'They treated us really well in America and we've made a lot of friends over there. Dr Epstein is pleased with Ashley's progress. It's been brilliant.

'Ashley's main concern now is to get home to see his brother and sister.'

After the Press conference they returned home to Northfleet, Kent. Once again Inspector Jan Berry, who had spearheaded the 'Ashley to America' campaign, became their taxi driver.

When they arrived they were delighted to see the house covered in banners, balloons and streamers to welcome Ashley home. There were lots of people waiting outside for them, including Simon and Michelle, and dozens of neighbours.

After two months apart, the wait proved too much for Simon and Michelle. 'The car carrying their world-famous little brother Ashley pulled up outside their banner-and-balloon-strewn house,' wrote Jane Millington of *Kent Today*. 'And the little brother and sister rushed forward to wrench open the car door and fling themselves inside.

'Parents Andrew and Vivien Fowle laughingly struggled to disentangle themselves from the riot of hugs and kisses. Six-year-old Michelle was shouting above the din to make sure no one missed the huge banner she had helped prepare.

' "Look, Ashley! It says: *Welcome Home!*" '

'While relatives, friends and intrigued passers-by who had gathered to watch the reunion struggled to hold back the tears, Ashley took it all in his stride. Beaming happily for the cameras he even joked: "I'm a star!" '

Among those waiting was Ashley's grandad Charlie Webb. He noticed how much weight Andrew had put on since being in New York.

By now Andrew and Vivien were so tired they couldn't fully appreciate the reunion. All they wanted to do was get into the house and collapse into bed. They were a bit annoyed that what had been intended as a private reunion with their other two children turned into such a public one.

At Gatwick they had made an agreement with the Press that they would hold a Press conference and that would be the end of things. But some of the less scrupulous Press decided to follow Jan Berry's car all the way to the house. Then they took pictures of the tearful reunion. Worse still, once they were all inside, the Press came up to the living room windows and took clandestine pictures of them. They just wouldn't leave Ashley alone.

'We put a banner up saying: "Welcome home, Ashley," ' recalled Simon later. 'Everyone was happy. Jackie said it was a miracle. We all sat in the house and had drinks. Then, when everyone had gone home, we had a celebration.'

After a lunch of spaghetti bolognese that Andrew's sister Angie had cooked, Vivien wanted to go out and buy something new to wear. They had been asked to go to Birmingham that night to appear on the TV show 'Good Morning... with Anne and Nick' the following morning. Vivien didn't dare go out of the front door, because the Press were waiting to pounce. Instead, she got on the phone: 'Dad, can you please take me into town? I'll come out the back. Can you pick me up from there?'

Meanwhile, the Press had gone up and down the row of terraced houses where the Fowle family lived asking people if they could use their back gardens. At least one journalist offered £20 to a neighbour for a privileged position. When Vivien went out of the back, the cameras started clicking away. The Press didn't even think to use the service road that runs along the back!

In the end, Andrew and Vivien let just one TV camera crew, BBC South East, into the house to do an interview. The station had been helpful to Andrew and Vivien, and they wanted to return the favour.

Later that afternoon the whole family were taken to Meridian Television studios in Maidstone and appeared on their evening news programme. They were then driven to a pub restaurant for a meal. From there they were picked up by a BBC driver and taken the 130 miles to Birmingham.

They arrived in Birmingham a little before midnight and went to their hotel. Andrew and Vivien collapsed into bed. The three children had managed to get some sleep on the long trip. But there was little chance of sleep for the parents. They were all up again at 5.30a.m. and were driven to the studio at Pebble Mill, just outside Birmingham city centre.

Initially, the BBC television people had intended to have Simon and Michelle appear on the programme along with the rest of the family. They had travelled all the way to Birmingham specially for the interview. But it wasn't to be. There just wasn't enough room on the sofa! As so often happened, Ashley was given VIP treatment and the media left out the two older children.

The interview with Anne Diamond and Nick Owen went well. Although they were tired, Andrew and Vivien expressed thanks to the millions of TV viewers.

Little Ashley spent much of the interview sticking his tongue out and making funny faces as he watched the monitor in front of him. When he was asked about turning on the Christmas tree lights in Walt Disney World, he got tongue-tied with the words 'pixie dust'. After his dad corrected him he repeated the words 'Pixie dust, pixie dust' over and over, to the delight of both presenters and viewers.

Off camera, Ashley said of Walt Disney World: 'It was wonderful. I met Mickey and all his friends and I sat on Donald Duck's lap. I really liked the colour of the Christmas tree.' Ashley recalled Dr Epstein saying to him: 'What a character you are.'

Later, Simon, Michelle and Ashley each received a photograph of Goofy signed by the character's voice, Bill Farmer.

While they were at Pebble Mill they met actress Michelle Collins, who played Cindy, Ian Beale's partner, in 'EastEnders'. When they walked into the make-up room she was sitting having her make-up done. Andrew said to her: 'We'd like you to meet another Michelle—Michelle Fowle.'

After the interview they were driven all the way home to Kent. They now had just two days to prepare for Christmas, and Vivien hadn't even started. She had said to her parents earlier in the year, months before they knew about Ashley's operation: 'Do you want to come to us for Christmas Day?' The arrangement still stood, and Andrew and Vivien somehow had to make it through Christmas.

Meanwhile, there was the huge task of getting family life back into some semblance of order. After the tension of the last few months, all they wanted to do was collapse in a heap. But life had to go on. Andrew needed to get back to work and Vivien had to learn again how to be a mother to three children instead of just one.

Simon and Michelle were finding it difficult to adjust to a normal routine after eight weeks' separation. 'Angie let us stay up this late,' they would say, or: 'We didn't have to put things away when Angie was here.'

Finally, Vivien put her foot down. 'Angie does things her way and I do them my way. This is how I want them done,' she said firmly.

Simon and Michelle—the children the Press forgot—could hardly remember anything before Ashley's illness. Much of their lives had been filled with news of their little brother's tragic illness.

The week before Ashley and his parents had flown to New York, Michelle had been crying while some friends were around for Hallowe'en.

'What's wrong, Michelle?' asked her dad.

'I don't want Ashley to die!' she wept.

After seeing their parents and Ashley off in the car, they had gone back into the house and cried.

'Don't worry,' Angie assured them. 'They'll be back soon.'

Naturally they found the eight weeks' separation from their parents very difficult to cope with. They watched the news of Ashley on TV with great interest and cut out items from the newspapers.

Simon was sad and missed Ashley. He cried at school and was sent to the first-aid room until he was able to cope with his classes. He felt better when he saw his little brother on TV. Simon believed his school work suffered badly because of the separation. He often lay awake at night, praying and hoping Ashley would get better.

'I was cross because they were all away so long and they couldn't take me,' he said. He had been worried in case Ashley and their parents wouldn't be back in time for Christmas.

Michelle, on the other hand, thought her parents would come back alone. 'I was surprised when they came back with Ashley,' she recalled. 'I kept having dreams about Ashley dying and about me going to his funeral.'

'I'm really glad that Ashley's at home now and that God's going to make him get better,' said nine-year-old Simon. 'I know his brain tumour won't come back because God won't let that happen. I like playing with Ashley. I enjoy doing anything he likes. I'd cry my eyes out if he died.'

Both Simon and Michelle at times wondered if their little brother was loved more than they were. 'The mother has to take care of the one who's sick more than the other two,' explained Simon. 'He needs more care than the others because he might be poorly.'

On Christmas Eve the whole family, with Ashley as guest of honour, spent an hour and a half at Thames-side Fire Station, Northfleet, Kent. The fire fighters there had supported the fundraising efforts, and they presented Ashley with a toy fire engine. The Fowles only left after an emergency call-out forced officers to excuse themselves.

On Boxing Day a large photograph of Ashley in his Superman suit filled page five of the *Daily Mail*. 'Superboy Ashley's Day of Delight,' the headline declared.

'Having my son home for Christmas is the best present I've ever had,' Andrew was quoted as saying. 'He loved the day. Every morning he has been asking: "What day is it today?" and when I finally told him "Christmas Day" his eyes just lit up—it was wonderful to see.'

Apart from his Superman outfit, Ashley's Christmas presents had included a new battery-operated computer and an Action Man with a big gun, a miniature version of the one he had wanted to use on the journalists at Gatwick Airport.

Vivien was glad when the clock struck midnight on 31 December 1994. It was the end of one of the worst years she had ever known. Now she looked ahead with the hope that Ashley's tumour would never return.

17 *Diary of Hope*

Ashley took his first steps in the New Year of 1995. Since he had returned to England from the US he had been having daily physiotherapy sessions to strengthen his arms and legs. He had begun to crawl and was now learning to walk again. Before the operation his arms would buckle under his own weight so he couldn't move about at all.

His doctor at the surgery, Dr Ian Millar, took out Ashley's stitches from his neck wound and ceremoniously presented them to him sealed in a couple of urine sample bottles. 'These are my blue spiders,' he told people proudly.

On Tuesday 10 January 1995 four-year-old Ashley was dressed up in his new maroon school uniform and left the house for his first day at Raynehurst Infants School in Gravesend, Kent. It was a day his parents had thought might never happen.

Outside the house there was the inevitable crowd of journalists, plying the family with questions. True to form, Ashley put them in their place, this time playing brilliantly to the cameras.

'Knock, knock,' he said.

'Who's there?'

'Scott.'

'Scott who?' asked the hardened journalists.

'Scott nothing to do with you!' shouted Ashley, throwing his head back with a roar of laughter.

'He's been really excited about this for weeks,' his dad proudly told the Press as Ashley boarded the school minibus. 'It'll be wonderful for him simply to mix with other children and lead a normal life again.'

Ashley started with half-days in the reception class, which was being taught by deputy head Jane Bright.

It was now clear that the surgery and drugs had not affected Ashley's intelligence. Tests before he started school showed he had the mental ability of a six-year-old.

The one problem Andrew and Vivien had was that the steroids Ashley had been taking since radiotherapy had caused his face and neck to swell. He had a thirteen-inch neck and they found it impossible to get shirts that size for him. He had to be content with a polo neck sweater instead.

At around the same time, *Kent Today* did a centre-page spread featuring Vivien. Called 'Ashley Mum's Diary of Hope', the feature was publicized on large posters outside newsagents throughout Kent.

By now the doctors in England were realizing that Ashley was much better than before. Soon after the operation Fred Epstein had written to Dr William Charlesworth, consultant in public health medicine for West Kent Health Authority, about the radiation therapy and steroids: 'Even at Ashley's young age, a full course of radiation therapy was given. Despite this, Ashley has continued to weaken and was on chronic steroids for some months.

'At the time of admission to this facility, he was quadriparetic, barely able to support his own weight and obviously Cushingoid as a result of long-term cortico-steroids.'

He went on to discuss the success or otherwise of the operation: 'Clearly, in a child, success is not simply surviving an operation or extending life by six months or a year or two. It requires a much longer symptom-free survival with a good quality of life to interpret the results of our efforts as a "success".

'I can only state that it has been my general experience that if I carry out an operation similar to the one done on Ashley, 90 per cent of patients have been alive without evidence of progression of the tumour five years later.'

His advice in the case of brain-stem tumours was to avoid radiotherapy, which tended to cause the tumour to swell, causing pressure on the nerve cells. The brain stem in a small child was tiny and any swelling could cause major problems. There should be surgery first; then, if necessary, radiotherapy afterwards, he said.

On Friday, 27 January Dr Grainne Evans, consultant community paediatrician at the Child Development Centre in Dartford, Kent, wrote a favourable report on Ashley's progress. Despite Ashley's physical difficulties, including walking with an unsteady ataxic gait and difficulty using his right hand, Dr Evans was happy.

'Ashley remains a friendly, open, trusting child with a lot of natural charm,' the paediatrician wrote. 'He gave very good visual and auditory attention to all material and has a good short-term memory. He is very well motivated, realistically confident and learns rapidly from experience.'

Although Ashley had a breath-holding fit while being examined physically, Dr Evans saw him as a child 'with above average ability' whose performance was constrained by his disabilities. 'Emotionally he is a very secure child in spite of his extensive surgery on another continent, which is testament to the loving care provided by his parents.'

Now that Andrew and Vivien were back in England, they had to find a specialist for Ashley. If he ever needed further surgery they had already decided to travel back to Dr Epstein. But for Ashley's ongoing care, they needed a specialist this side of the Atlantic they could trust. They felt reluctant to return to Guy's.

They phoned Fred Epstein in New York.

'Who do we turn to?' asked Andrew. 'Have you got any recommendations?'

'Try Anthony Hockley at Birmingham Children's Hospital.'

They made an appointment with Anthony Hockley in February 1995. He looked at Ashley and they showed him the MRI scans done soon after the operation.

'Do you think you could have done this operation?' asked Andrew.

Anthony Hockley, the specialist neurosurgeon at Birmingham Children's Hospital, sat back in his chair for a moment, reflecting. As he sat there, Vivien thought how much he looked like the soccer goalkeeper Gordon Banks.

'Yes, of course I could have done it,' he replied at last.

'Would you be willing to see Ashley regularly?'

'Yes, I'd be willing to take on Ashley's case,' he said. 'But do you *really* want all this travelling every time you come to see me? Wouldn't you prefer somewhere closer to home?'

'We would, but we don't know where to go. Dr Epstein's recommended you, saying you're probably the best in the country. We're happy to come to Birmingham each time. We travelled all the way to New York!'

'What about Richard Hayward at Great Ormond Street Hospital?'

When they arrived back home they phoned Fred Epstein again.

'Richard Hayward? Yeah, I know him. We write to each other regularly. He's OK.'

As a result they decided to make an appointment with Richard Hayward. But before they could attend the appointment they met him in a different context—an emergency.

In February 1995 they rushed Ashley to Great Ormond Street Hospital in London. He appeared to be a very ill little boy. He had been getting headaches and was being sick. These were the symptoms Andrew and Vivien were told to expect if his shunt became blocked. Fred Epstein had warned that this might happen because after an operation the blood in the cerebrospinal fluid tends to congeal and sometimes blocks the shunt.

The doctors at the hospital ran various tests—blood, urine and a spinal tap to extract some cerebrospinal fluid from the central nervous system. At one point they suspected meningitis. In the end it turned out to be a virus infection, not a blocked shunt.

During this visit they met Richard Hayward, the specialist paediatric neurosurgeon. Andrew and Vivien knew his name because after Ashley's operation he told the Press that he could have performed the same operation in England. They showed him Ashley's scans from New York.

Richard Hayward spoke with a posh accent, and bore a vague similarity to Christopher Lee, the star of many of the Dracula films. After looking at the scans he said: 'You've obviously been to the best surgeon in the world for this kind of tumour. Fred's done a very good job.'

Andrew asked him what he thought the future held for Ashley.

His reply totally shocked them both. 'The long-term prognosis still isn't very good, I'm afraid.'

Yet again they were devastated by a British doctor's negative attitude towards Ashley's condition. They went home in shock and phoned Fred Epstein straight away.

Dr Epstein was furious. 'Ask Richard Hayward what experience he's got with this type of tumour. I can't make any guarantees to you that Ashley—or you, for that matter—will live. You might walk under a bus tomorrow. What I *can* say is that I've been doing this operation for five or six years now and fifteen out of the seventeen patients with identical tumours to your son's I operated on five years ago are still alive with no regrowth of their tumours. In my book, those are pretty good odds.'

'Well, I know you don't give any guarantees, but at least you give us hope, confidence and determination,' said Vivien. 'To be honest, we feel totally fed up when we've been to hospitals here in England. We're meant to be seeing Richard Hayward regularly for Ashley's check-ups, but if we don't have faith in what he's telling us, what's the point?'

'Do you want me to write to this doctor?' Fred Epstein asked. 'No, heck, I'm *going* to write him!''

Several weeks later, Vivien was speaking to Dr Epstein's secretary on the phone.

'I don't know what you said to Fred that time,' she recalled. 'He was fuming mad after your phone call. I had to go around picking up all the medical books he slung around the room. Boy, does it take a lot for Fred to get mad!'

Whatever Fred Epstein wrote in his letter seemed to do the trick. After that Richard Hayward was very different in his attitude.

Ashley recovered quickly from his illness. The doctors put it down to a forty-eight-hour virus that was made worse because his body's own immune system was low because of the steroids and radiotherapy he had previously received. By March Ashley had stopped taking steroids and all other medication except vitamin supplements.

In a letter to Dr Joan Whitehead, the consultant oncologist, Fred Epstein had expressed the need to wean Ashley off steroids because his immune system was depressed. Fred was concerned that because of Ashley's young age there could be long-term scoliosis (curvature of the spine), as well as possible thyroid dysfunction and radiation myelitis.

Dr Whitehead was the one who had said the doctors were regularly in touch with Dr Epstein and that he was embarrassed by the *Reader's Digest* articles. On 11 April she wrote to Andrew and Vivien concerning questions they had raised in the Press about the way they had been misinformed at Guy's Hospital.

'I would have expected and did presume that Dr Epstein might well have been embarrassed by some of the claims and the style in which they were made by others on his behalf,' she wrote. 'However, looking at the article now, I realize I was wrong in my presumption.'

She described their allegation that she had lied as 'an ungracious accusation calculated to cast a gratuitous and undeserved slur on my character and my professional standing'. And she asked them to 'withdraw the unpleasant allegation against me'.

Even though, as Christians, Andrew and Vivien had forgiven Dr Whitehead, they wanted to make sure that other parents in the future would be given the full range of options for their children. They therefore decided to pursue a possible legal action and passed on Dr Whitehead's letter to their lawyer.

On Thursday 22 April the whole Fowle family went on a day trip to France on board the ferry *Stena Challenger* as the captain and crew's guests of honour. Fred Stokes, the head steward, showed them round the ship. The ferry company Stena Sealink, whose vessel *Challenger* travels the English Channel several times each day, had been enthusiastic supporters of the 'Ashley to America' appeal. The ship's crew had even raised £150 for the appeal during a force-eight gale!

Andrew wrote to thank them afterwards: 'Words can't express the gratitude we feel towards you all, because although Dr Epstein performed the miracle of surgery, you are all responsible for giving Ashley this chance of life. We'll be eternally grateful to you for what you achieved for our son.'

The time was drawing close for Ashley's first MRI scan since the operation six months previously. Although Andrew and Vivien's immediate worries were over, they still had the underlying fear that part of the tumour remained in Ashley's brain stem. 'What if it starts growing again and can't be removed surgically?' Vivien thought.

Jackie, her sister, said she believed the miracle wasn't over yet; God had more work to do. Whatever that meant, Vivien knew that all they could do was wait.

They kept their appointment with Richard Hayward at Great Ormond Street Hospital. In silence he held up Ashley's new scans.

'Well, I can't see any active tumour,' he said.

'How much tumour's left?' asked Vivien.

'That's what I'm saying,' he said. 'I just can't see any at all!'

Richard Hayward was over the moon about the result. He said it was a combination of the radiotherapy in the UK and the surgery in the US that had resulted in the tumour apparently disappearing completely.

Richard Hayward wrote to Fred Epstein after seeing Ashley at his clinic. 'Ashley continues to make excellent neurological progress,' he wrote. 'He is walking on his own for a few paces and the right-sided weakness that was so prominent before has now improved greatly.

'Now to the MRI scan. You will be delighted to hear

that the new images show no clear evidence of an active tumour. The ventricles are only moderately enlarged, suggesting that the shunt system is continuing to work well.'

Fred Epstein was sent copies of the scans and confirmed Richard Hayward's conclusion, though as usual he erred on the side of caution.

'I'm 200 per cent happier than I thought I would be at this stage,' he told Andrew. 'But I know I left 5 to 10 per cent of the tumour in there.'

He supported Richard Hayward's cautious approach. 'I'm not surprised at his initial sceptical reaction,' said Fred Epstein when Andrew phoned him. 'My methods aren't accepted by doctors even in some parts of my own country. But I'm glad he can see the results, though I don't agree that the radiotherapy had any effect on the tumour.'

Once Dr Epstein had spoken with Andrew and Vivien they allowed themselves to rejoice. The tumour that had plagued their lives for most of 1994 and half of 1995, and that had threatened Ashley's life like a loaded gun pointed at his head, had disappeared without trace. Nothing remained of it—no scar tissue, nothing. It was as if it had never been there.

The miracle was complete. God, they believed—through Fred Epstein's skills—had healed their son.

18 Superboy Meets Wolf

As time went on, Andrew and Vivien kept in regular contact with Dr Fred Epstein, phoning him every couple of months with a progress report on Ashley. Like a lot of parents of his former patients, they were given his home phone number and he invited them to call him at any time if they had a worry.

One Sunday morning at about 10 o'clock Andrew decided to ring him, forgetting that the time difference in New York made it five o'clock in the morning local time. A very sleepy neurosurgeon mumbled 'Hello' into the receiver.

'Hi, Dr Epstein. It's Andrew Fowle here, Ashley's dad. Er—did I get you out of bed?'

'Well, it *is* rather early over here,' came the understated reply.

On Sunday, 23 July 1995, Ashley had his fifth birthday party at the Tudor Park Hotel, Bearsted, near Maidstone in Kent. The host, Sanjay, was helpful and patient. Ashley's family and friends included thirty-eight children and two people who had been closely involved in the 'Ashley to America' appeal, Inspector Jan Berry and Jill Clements, as well as Sue Roberton, the Police Welfare officer who went with Andrew and Vivien on the trip to the US.

Angie Fowle helped to entertain all the children with games. Then there was the food. The hotel chef and kitchen staff had laid on a delicious spread of food. Unlike his fourth party, when he couldn't eat a thing, Ashley tucked in as enthusiastically as the rest of the children.

Before the party started Vivien told the crowds of waiting Press that he had made excellent progress towards a full recovery and was now attending school full time. 'He gets mood swings because he can't do what normal children do,' she said. 'He still can't go upstairs or dress himself—but we'll get there.'

For months he had woken to a breakfast of steroids, digestion pills and sickness drugs. He had also been on a low-salt, sweet-free and high protein diet. Now all his medication had stopped and Ashley had returned to his normal average height and weight for a five-year-old.

The hotel gave Ashley a pile of presents. So did the crew of *Stena Challenger*. All the children enjoyed the party and went home exhausted. The adults were exhausted, too!

During the summer holidays Ashley had his head shaved. By now he was wearing a back brace because of his curved spine, and shaving his head was a way of cooling him down in the heatwave. Ashley said he liked his new look.

The whole family, including Ashley, took part in the Northfleet Carnival, dressing up as clowns and raising money for the Rainbow Trust. Jackie painted rainbows all over her car. That proved a problem afterwards. Even though she had only used poster paint, it would come off only with a lot of hard rubbing using a solvent.

Death was a subject that became very important that summer, especially now that Ashley was out of immediate danger. The Fowle children's great-grandmother died and Simon went to the funeral and then to the reception afterwards. He found the funeral quite upsetting especially when the coffin 'went into the big oven'.

Then their hamster died. Ashley had been shown several times on TV playing with the family ginger-and-white hamster, Dudley. All three children were sad when it later died.

Even though they had never met her, all three children were deeply upset by the news that Chelsea Burke, another child with a brain tumour, had died in August that year.

The series of deaths resulted in Simon and Michelle thinking more about their little sister Elizabeth's cot death before either of them were born. A photograph of Elizabeth sat on their TV and they often wondered what she was like. The bit Simon didn't like was the news about his little sister's autopsy. 'They cut Elizabeth open and checked if there were any dangerous things,' he said bluntly.

On a brighter note, the Starlight Foundation had been set up to grant wishes for seriously ill children. In August 1995 it arranged for Ashley and his family to meet the TV superheroes, the Gladiators, including Ashley's special hero, Wolf.

'I just wish you could have seen Ashley's face when he realized we were going to see the Gladiators,' Andrew wrote to the Starlight Foundation. 'We managed to keep it a secret right up until we arrived at the main doors of the arena, even though there were lots of people walking around the city carrying the large yellow-foam Glad hands.

'The show was great, and we managed to get ringside seats. After the show we went back stage where we met Wolf. Ashley was thrilled and even got a kiss and a cuddle from Wolf himself. I must admit it brought a tear to my eye when Ashley looked up into Wolf's face and said: "I love you."

'We left the arena and walked back to the hotel, getting lost on the way. When we finally walked into the foyer at about 12.20a.m. we couldn't believe it. All the Gladiators were staying in the same hotel as us. There they were, sitting around chatting. I'd like to thank you for making our children so happy. They all deserved it as they've put up with a lot over the last year and a half.

'One more favour. I'd dearly like to write a letter to Wolf and thank him personally for sparing the time to make Ashley's day. I don't think he'll ever realize how much seeing him actually meant to Ashley.'

Ashley was due to have another six-monthly MRI scan on 6 November 1995. The pressure increased for Andrew and Vivien as the time for Ashley's six-monthly scan drew closer. Vivien tended to get panic attacks while Andrew got very tense.

Because it was a year after Ashley's operation, he was followed into hospital by the media, including a TV crew from the BBC South East newsroom.

Great Ormond Street Hospital for Sick Children is situated in the heart of London. A taxi took the family to the front door. From there they walked a few steps along a glass-covered walkway to the modern, refurbished reception. Great Ormond Street is world-famous because J.M. Barrie, the author of *Peter Pan*, bequeathed the royalties from his book to the ongoing care of sick children there. As a result, much of the hospital features aspects of the book.

In the reception area is the modern Peter Pan canteen. The wards are named after animals, and visitors follow the footprints of a particular animal through the corridors to where they need to go. If they are going to Elephant Ward, for instance, they follow the large elephant footprints. Ashley and his parents were heading for Parrot Ward, following the four-clawed bird footprints to the third floor in a fairly new part of the hospital.

Once the MRI scan had been done they had a tense ten days' wait for the results. What if the tumour had started to grow back? Would they have to go through the ordeal of a major operation yet again?

There was no trace at all of the tumour. 'If I could design a scan for Ashley's spinal cord and brain stem, this is exactly how I'd have designed it,' declared Richard Hayward, Great Ormond Street's neurosurgeon.

Meanwhile Ashley was walking much better and doing well at school. The only slight problems were a tilt of his head and curvature of the spine, problems that can be corrected surgically when he is older. He had to wear a back brace during the daytime and was being given regular exercises to strengthen his neck muscles.

The media, always interested in anniversaries, highlighted Ashley's success story so far. They were particularly interested in the forthcoming book about the battle to get help for Ashley.

On 25 November 1995 Ashley was the special guest who switched on the Christmas lights in the town of West Malling, Kent. The media were there, and posters had been put up around the town with the words: 'Lights switching on ceremony by Ashley Fowle aged $5^1/_2$ assisted by Sir John Stanley MP aged 53 $^3/_4$.'

Ashley had switched on the lights at Walt Disney World, Orlando, the previous year. 'We wanted an expert and Ashley fits the bill,' declared Bob Ansell, chairman of the Malling and District Chamber of Commerce. 'He's an obvious choice.'

Wearing a pair of red antlers, Ashley flicked the switch. As the street lit up, the Rev. Brian Stevenson, vicar of St Mary the Virgin church, led the carol singing.

Vivien used the occasion to tell the media about the latest all-clear on Ashley's MRI scan. 'This justifies our decision to take him to New York last November,' she said. 'He's now toilet-trained, which we were told he never could be, and he can walk. His speech is very good. In fact, he has a fluency in advance of his years.'

The organizers of the West Malling event bought Ashley a Playmobil castle. Determined not to leave out the others, they gave Simon a geometry and pen set and Michelle yet another doll, though by now she no longer pulled off her dolls' heads!

Boxing Day brought Christmas 1995 to an exciting ending when Ashley, together with his brother Simon and sister Michelle, met the players of Premier League soccer team West Ham.

Ashley's involvement in the club began back in November 1994 when BBC Radio Kent held an auction for the 'Ashley to America' appeal. Matthew Liston, a civilian working at Maidstone Police Station, had driven round all the Premier League soccer clubs, asking them to donate a signed ball, shirt or other item to offer at the auction. All except Chelsea responded. Of them all, West Ham was the most generous. They gave various items for the auction as well as a scarf, hat and other supporters' souvenirs for Ashley to keep.

Andrew said jokingly to Ashley at the time: 'You're going to have to support West Ham now because they've been so good to you.'

Ashley, however, took it to heart. From then on he became an ardent West Ham fan. While he was in New York he kept his West Ham scarf draped across the top of his hospital bed. Back in the UK, during one interview on the national breakfast TV programme GMTV (Good Morning Television), he was asked by Eamon Holmes: 'What soccer team do you support?'

'West Ham,' Ashley replied brightly.

'Oh, dear. Well, Ashley, you're going to have to have another operation to cure you of that!' replied Eamon.

Simon and Michelle hadn't appeared on the show, but they had been able to watch the whole thing from just behind the cameras. They kept making faces into the monitors. Then they were taken into the control room and given VIP treatment. They had two sticky buns each at the end of the show. Best of all for them, they had the rest of the day off school, going to their grandparents' house instead.

The next day GMTV phoned to say that Brian Nicholls of West Ham had been on the phone, wanting Ashley to meet the players. Ashley's family were invited as special guests at the big match against Coventry on Boxing Day 1995. The plan was to kit Ashley in the team colours and take him out onto the pitch as the team mascot.

As it turned out, the groundsmen had forgotten to put covers over the pitch the previous night and the ground was frozen solid. It was too dangerous to play, and 22,000 disappointed ticketholders were sent home.

That didn't stop Ashley meeting the players, including his two favourites, Julian Dicks and Tony Cottee. As the cameras whirred, Ashley said to Julian: 'I'm going to take your place!' The team presented Ashley with soccer kit, real goalkeepers' gloves and a book of autographs. Despite the disappointment about not being a mascot, Ashley had a great time. So did his brother Simon, another West Ham supporter.

The story was featured on GMTV the following morning.

By January 1996 Ashley was climbing the stairs by himself, closely followed by big brother Simon, the boy-catcher extraordinaire.

Andrew and Vivien see a bright future for Ashley. 'I can't help thinking he's going to be someone important when he's older,' says Andrew.

At the same time there are the nagging questions: Is the tumour going to grow back? Will he be able to walk properly on his own? Will he get enough dexterity in his hands to feed himself?

They believe God is going to use him. People have brought messages about this. He also has a spiritual insight beyond his years. While going through the radiotherapy treatment Ashley, then aged three and a half, woke up one weekend morning in bed at home and looked into Andrew's eyes.

'Guess what, Dad?' he said, his face beaming. 'In my dreams Jesus told me I'm going to be healed.'

'I can't see him dying young,' says Andrew. 'I can imagine him living to a ripe old age. How well he'll be physically, I just don't know.

'Our biggest regret is that we didn't go to Fred Epstein sooner and that we let Ashley have the radio-therapy. If only we'd been more forceful about getting his scans sent to the US earlier, he would never have been given the radiotherapy. Perhaps he'd have been a lot stronger and less disabled.

'But then, if he'd never had the radiotherapy, the urgency wouldn't have been there to get him over to the US because the tumour would have stayed relatively stable.'

It's hard to tell whether Ashley's shunt is still needed or not. If the cerebrospinal fluid is flowing and the shunt is still working properly, Ashley may get negative pressure in his head. The shunt isn't doing any harm. If the doctors took it out and he still needed it, he would have to go through the same ordeal again.

A girl in the bed next to Ashley's when he was in the Maudsley Hospital, London, also had a shunt. The doctors thought she didn't need it and took it out. She then had so much pain as a result of headaches that they had to put in a second shunt. After all Ashley has been through, Andrew and Vivien don't want him going through an ordeal like that.

Ever since Ashley's operation, Andrew and Vivien have planned to return to New York with the whole family to visit the friends they made there. Their two oldest children, Simon and Michelle, want to meet Fred Epstein, the great surgeon who saved their little brother's life.

Simon has a particular reason for meeting him because they share something in common. Ashley's problems resulted in huge upheavals and disruptions during Simon's formative years. As a result, he has always struggled with school work. Similarly, Fred Epstein had learning difficulties as a boy, yet went on to become one the world's greatest neurosurgeons. Simon says he wants to find out how Fred did it so he can achieve something with his own life.

Who knows what the future holds for Ashley Fowle? Perhaps one day his whole life's story will be told to millions of TV viewers.

His parents like to imagine the scene. The titles come up for the British TV show 'This is Your Life' and a middle-aged Phillip Schofield tells the audience about the unsuspecting subject of that week.

The scene changes to Ashley walking proudly with only a slight limp, using a walking-stick instead of the crutches or wheelchair a person with his level of disability would be expected to use. Family and friends tell their part of his amazing, super story.

Dee comes on, a red-haired nurse from the Maudsley Hospital, a favourite of Ashley's—now with grey hair.

Then an old, white-haired American neurosurgeon comes out from behind stage, grins broadly and walks to the front, waving his hands in the air to acknowledge the roar of applause.

'I'm Dr Epstein,' he says. 'I promised your parents I'd help you, Ashley. And I sure didn't let them down.'

Appendix

What happened to the money?

Over £80,000 was raised for the 'Ashley to America' appeal. Most of it came in during the first three days, but money continued to trickle in after the appeal was officially closed.

Some questions have been raised in the Press about what happened to the money left over after all the bills for Ashley's operation had been settled.

The original estimate of costs for the operation was $47,500. It was made up of $28,000 for the hospital stay, $15,000 for Fred Epstein's fee, $2,500 for the anaesthetist and $2,000 for the consultant physician.

In the event there were quite a number of additional expenses, some of them totally unexpected. Visiting consultants who examined Ashley even for a few moments sent in invoices long after the Fowle family had returned to the UK. Most of these were for $200 to $500. The American medical insurance system meant that the doctors were dependent for their income on charging for contact with patients. Most American citizens are covered by medical insurance. That wasn't the case with Ashley, so they felt free to ask their normal fee.

Ashley's second unexpected return to hospital when he developed an infection resulted in additional costs, including a $5,000 invoice from the plastic surgeon. That brought the total to $60,000.

After these costs and all the other expenses of the trip were met, some £36,000 was left to be put into Ashley's trust fund. The trustees of the account plan for the money to stay there until the doctors and Andrew and Vivien agree that it is unlikely that he will ever need further treatment for his brain stem and spinal cord.

It is written into the trust that, once Andrew and Vivien and the doctors agree that Ashley is likely to need no further treatment, the money will be split and distributed to children's charities of their choice. These could include the Rainbow Trust and Ronald McDonald Children's Charities. They will also probably give some money back to the Alex Barret Fund which gave Ashley £2,500. They have been told that if the tumour doesn't recur within five years it is unlikely ever to grow again. They will probably wait six or seven years to be on the safe side.

Another possible way forward is to keep the trust open and fund equipment for hospitals or for individual children or to pay to send children to other countries for specialized treatment.

Brain and spinal cord tumours

In Britain each year about 180 to 200 children are newly diagnosed as having brain and spinal cord tumours. Of these only one or two are in the brain stem.

Persistent headaches, especially in the mornings, accompanied by nausea and vomiting, together possibly with mental confusion, could be a sign of a brain tumour. Other signs could include disturbed vision, impaired speech and hearing, drowsiness, reduced movement, loss of balance and personality changes.

Sometimes the person gets seizures, often known as fits or convulsions. These can vary in intensity and are due to a build-up of abnormal electrical activity in the brain when nerve cells are irritated by a brain tumour. Ashley had other symptoms of a brain-stem tumour. These included weakness in his arms and legs, stumbling or lack of co-ordination in walking (ataxic gait), and abnormal eye movements and changes in vision.

Diagnosing a brain- or spinal-cord tumour can be complex. The neurologist or neurosurgeon tests the nervous system by checking the power and strength of arms and legs, knee reflexes, ability to feel pinpricks and telling the difference between hot and cold. The eyes are checked using an ophthalmoscope. This shines a light onto the retina (the lining of the eye) and the optic nerve, which connects the eye to the brain. A tumour resulting in introcranial pressure will cause part of the optic nerve to swell visibly.

The most common forms of brain tumour are the glionas, which affect the glial (supportive) tissue. An astrocytoma arises from small, star-shaped cells known as astrocytes. In adults they are confined mainly to the cerebrum; in children they occur in the brain stem and cerebellum as well as the cerebrum. A grade 3 astrocytoma is called *anaplastic astrocytoma*. A grade 4 one is called *glioblastoma multiforme*.

Ependymoma tumours occur most commonly in children and usually develop in the lining of the ventricles or the spinal cord.

Useful addresses

Ronald McDonald Children's Charities
11-59 High Road
East Finchley
London N2 8AW
Telephone: 0181-444 4564

The Evelina Family Trust
115-122 Snowsfield
London SE1 3SS
Telephone: 0171 955 4780
Raises funds to provide and manage the Ronald
McDonald House at Guy's for the use of families of
seriously ill children undergoing hospital treatment

BACUP
3 Bath Place
Rivington Street
London EC2A 3JR
Telephone from London: 0171-613 2121,
Outside London: 0800-181199
Counselling service: 0171-696 9000
Publishes *Children with Cancer: A Guide to Help for
Families,* containing details of more than eighty charities
and organizations offering help to parents of children
with cancer.

Rainbow Trust
Surrey House
31 Church Street
Leatherhead
Surrey KT22 8EF
Telephone: 01372-363438
Fax: 01372 363101
Offers domiciliary care twenty-four hours a day for
terminally-ill children and their families. Also provides
short-stay holiday accommodation in the countryside for
the families.

Association for Spina Bifida and Hydrocephalus
42 Park Road
Peterborough
Cambs PE1 2UQ
Telephone: 01733-555988
Offers field workers who can contact families and liaise
with other professionals involved with the family. Also
has advisers on living with disability

The Foundation for the Study of Infant Death
14, Halkin Street,
London
SW1X 7DP
Telephone: 0171 235 0965
Provides support for families whose baby has died,
including a 24-hour helpline (0171 235 1721), a
network of parent groups throughout the country, and
liaison with health professionals.